SEATTLE
COACH ®

CONNECTION. CURIOSITY.
CHALLENGE.

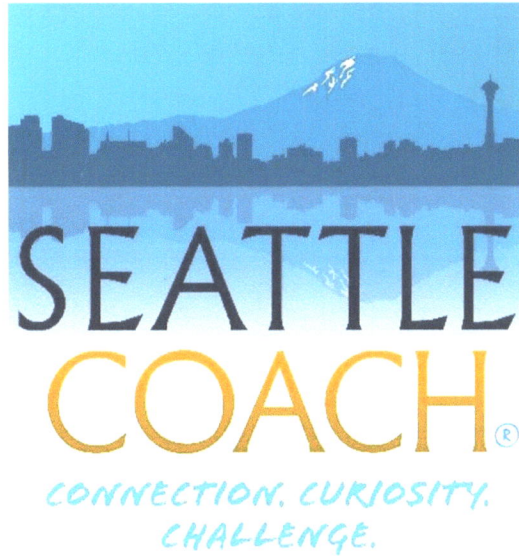

The Coaching for Leaders Playbook

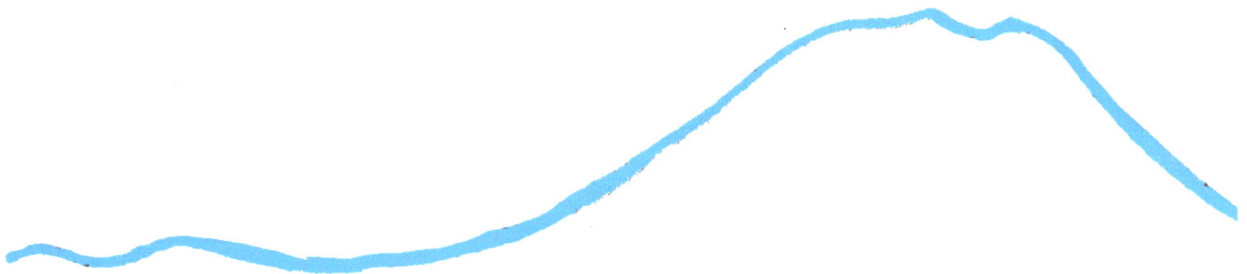

Doing the Craft. Being the Coach.

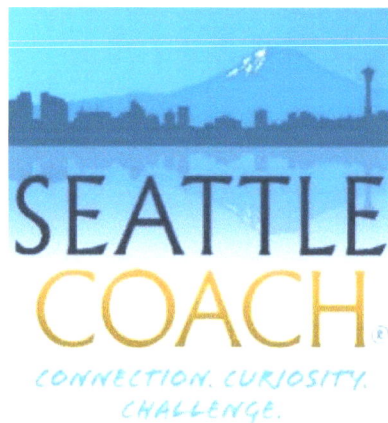

The Coaching for Leaders Playbook

Our goal is to scale with quality. Once you've completed one of our SeattleCoach Training and Development Cohorts and would like to license the use of some of our materials please contact us at the address below. We'll tell you how it works.

The SeattleCoach Professional Training & Development Company
2727 Fairview Ave East, Suite F
Seattle, WA 98102
206-412-6224
www.seattlecoach.com

Printed in the United States of America.
ISBN: 979-8-88797-084-4 (Paperback)

Library of Congress Control Number: 2023915840

The SeattleCoach Stash

As you open this book, you are likely a coaching leader who has joined an in-person or virtual **SeattleCoach Coaching for Leaders (CFL)** Cohort. In the coming months, our work together will include

1. Ten ninety-minute live general sessions;
2. Pre-session and post-session communications;
3. And between each general session, an hour of facilitated peer coaching with two or three of your fellow participants along with some independent study.

Or maybe you're reading this **Playbook** independently.

Either way, the QR code below will take you to the **SeattleCoach Stash (aka The Coaching for Leaders references and resources page).**

Here's how it works:

1. When you see *a numerical green superscript*, open the PDF that's linked at the top of **The Stash** to review external resources and references.
2. When you see *an orange superscript* *(alphabetical)*, find the corresponding SeattleCoach tool, work-sheet, video, or audio file listed on the page.

https://www.seattlecoach.com/seattlecoach-cfl-the-stash.html

As more and more leaders seek to add coaching skills, behaviors, and presence to their work, I'll post more resources in **The Stash**. Most resources will appear first in my newsletter, *Coachable!,* so when you point your camera at the QR code, one of the first things you'll see is a link to subscribe.

About *The Coaching for Leaders Playbook*

Through the years, we at SeattleCoach have trained hundreds of senior leaders in technology, healthcare,

faith communities, real estate, and other key sectors. Each one has become fluent in the skills, behaviors, and personal presence of coaching leadership.

Along the way, as we've learned from hundreds of SeattleCoaches and from the demands of this time in history, we have developed two proven SeattleCoach Training and Development tracks.

Track #1: Our Professional Certification Cohorts

In the spring of 2008, Patty Burgin began training small cohorts of mid-career professionals. In their own ways, each person had asked her some version of, "How do I learn to do what you do?" And each person was seeking certification in this emerging old/new profession of coaching. That same year SeattleCoach became a credentialed training provider of the International Coaching Federation (ICF). Since then, hundreds of mid-career executives have pursued the rigorous preparation required for professional certification. These small cohorts of allies have become known as SeattleCoach Flagship Cohorts.[a]

Track #2: "Coaching for Leaders" (CFL)

Then in 2015, leaders and their organizations began to ask us for executive coaching education for their veteran leaders. This track could be briefer and more customized. We listened and began to understand that this second wave would require three things:

1. *Sponsoring executives who understood the value of coaching;*
2. *Leaders and people-managers who were raising their hands; and*
3. *External executive coaches who knew how to facilitate and model the learning.*

In response, we co-created rich cohort experiences for organizational leaders and their teams. Rather than focusing on professional credentialing, these veteran leaders and their sponsors are aiming to increase their leadership effectiveness. They too are SeattleCoaches. And they are building world-class coaching cultures. We called this second wave "Coaching for Leaders" (CFL).[b]

SeattleCoach is the "craft brewery of leadership coaching." In everything we do, our goal is to start with world-class ingredients: our content, our process, and cohorts of people like you. Along the way we stay accessible and responsive, and we leave a coaching community of "Connection, Curiosity, and Challenge" in our wake. We charge for our work, but the affection is free.

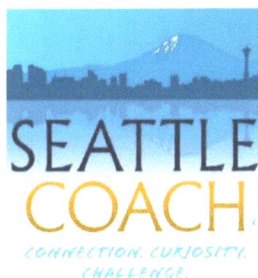

Welcome to "Coaching for Leaders" (CFL).

Through the culture quakes of the past few years, the demand for leaders who are fluent with the "coaching gear" is growing. It's a delight to me that though our work is increasingly virtual and national, SeattleCoach has kept our magic. We are still "the small craft brewery of coach training programs." And each of our participants knows that they belong to a tribe that is changing the world a little.

Life is big and life is short, and extraordinary coaching leaders remind me every day that I get to fill a huge chunk of mine doing something I am enthusiastic about. Each of our coaching leaders has made me a better coach and a better person. And they have helped make this edition of *The Coaching for Leaders Playbook* better than ever.

And this is a good place to acknowledge my extraordinary editor, Heidi King, at **Publish Your Purpose Press**. A great mind and a great heart—and when it comes time for you to start writing, I recommend her to you.

This *Playbook* is designed to be a stand-alone resource, but it's even richer (and more fun) if you move through its lessons and experiments in the company of allies in one of our SeattleCoach Cohorts.

In our journey together, we'll challenge and support you as you learn and experiment with key coaching skills and competencies and with human change management. In addition, you'll have opportunities to deeply examine your own life and leadership presence. As a member of one of our CFL Cohorts, you can expect to build lifelong friends and allies.

At SeattleCoach we've all been reminded that we're in this moment of history together, living and learning and grateful in the process of "doing the craft and being the coach." So, welcome to our unique tribe of coaches and to the larger twenty-first-century leadership movement that is professional coaching.

To the journey then!

Patricia Burgin, MA, MCC, LMFT
SeattleCoach Founder and CEO
Seattle, Washington

The SeattleCoach definition of leadership coaching

A collaborative—even elegant—conversation, of any length, that fosters a growth mindset by inviting the full dimensional intelligence and presence of the people involved.

Being asked a great question, and then being listened to well, lights up our brains in a way being told stuff never can. The coaching leader's goal is for the light to go on in the brain of the person he or she is in conversation with.

Coaching is the craft of effectively creating and delivering highly customized and collaborative, just-in-time adult learning and leadership development. —Patty Burgin

[On vocation] The place God calls you to is the place where your deep gladness and world's deep hunger meet. —Frederick Buechner

The big break for me was deciding that this was my life. —Jon Stewart

You rarely have time for everything you want in this life, so you need to make choices. And hopefully your choices can come from a deep sense of who you are. —Fred Rogers

I focus leaders on themselves rather than on their followers, and on the nature of their presence rather than on their technique and "know-how." —Edwin Friedman

If done well, coaching can elevate the productivity and performance of every individual in the organization. And there is a significant correlation between having a strong coaching culture and market performance. —Creating a Coaching Culture, Institute for Corporate Productivity

If you do not become cynical, if you work hard and are kind, amazing things will happen. —Conan O'Brien

I try to be alert and available. If you're not available, the sort of ordinary time goes past, and you didn't live it. But if you're available, life gets huge. —Bill Murray

The mind is not a vessel to be filled but a fire to be kindled. —Plutarch

Be kind to yourself. If being hard on yourself was going to work, it would have worked by now. —Jamie Smart

The Coaching for Leaders Playbook

Doing the Craft. Being the Coach.

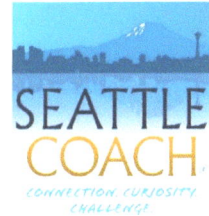

Where We're Headed in "Coaching for Leaders"

Introduction to "Coaching for Leaders"

Doing the Craft, Part 1

Coachability and Human Change

Doing the Craft, Part 2

Key Coaching Skills and Behaviors

Being the Coach

Your Coaching Presence: The Core of Coaching Leadership

The Appendix

About the Author /121

Introduction to "Coaching for Leaders"

Preparing for "Coaching for Leaders"

Whether you're working as a part of a Coaching for Leaders (CFL) Cohort or independently, we invite you to spend some time with the following questions. Some of them will make you pause and reflect, while others will be easier to answer. Taking time to think about your life, your strengths and values, your satisfaction, and your contribution is the best starting point for adding coaching skills and presence to the way you lead. Record some of your initial thoughts below—you'll probably need more room.

Your Life So Far

Your CFL Facilitator Coaches, will hold a steady focus on two things:

1. Helping you learn the skills and presence required in the craft of coaching, and
2. Helping you understand and refine how you will bring yourself, your gifts, and your strengths to your own version of being a coach or coaching leader. What are the gifts and strengths and stories that have always been core to your identity? What are the gifts and strengths and stories that might be ready to emerge at this point in your life?

What would you say have been your three greatest accomplishments to date?

1.

2.

3.

If you've been accepted into this program, you are already a seasoned leader. What do you see as your existing "craft" or area of true mastery? Write a little about how you can imagine using that expertise or understanding as you build competency as a coaching leader.

What major transitions have you experienced in the past two years? (Entering or approaching a new decade, a new relationship, leaving a soul-sucking job, moving toward a better one, a new role, a new residence, a loss, changes in children's ages/stages, becoming an "elder" in your professional world, etc.)

In our experience, part of developing as a great coaching leader is having or beginning to build a strong support system of people who know you and what you're up to, and with whom you can share your progress. Who are the people in your life who will be tracking with you as you develop your coaching skills and presence, and with whom you can share your insights and discoveries (managers, family members, friends, mentors, etc.)? As we begin, consider letting these people know about your best hopes as a member of this CFL Cohort.

Potential and Possibility

What are some of the goals and outcomes you are beginning to envision as a coaching leader?

Much of the richness of coaching and developing as a coach comes in finding a balance between reflecting and doing. For some of us this is where our spirituality is a resource. As you move into coach training, write a little about how you take time to reflect on your life and work. How do you course correct? Metabolize what you're learning? How and when do you create an environment that is conducive to your learning?

Your "Character Strengths"

Coaching is a highly strengths-based way of working, and we'd love to know some of your strengths as we get underway.

You may find it useful, even interesting to take a brief inventory. "The VIA Survey of Character"[1] is a free, well-researched assessment designed by researchers at the University of Pennsylvania to help people identify, develop, and then use their best character qualities in pursuit of their goals.

Because this is part of a research project, you will be asked to register, but the researchers won't spam you. After you register, click on the "VIA Survey" button to begin. When you've finished the survey, note your top five character strengths below. (No need to purchase a report unless you want to.) As we work together, we'll ask you to keep a copy of your top five character strengths in mind. For an eight-minute video summary of the thinking behind the project, watch the eight-minute YouTube video on "The Science of Character."[2]

1.

2.

3.

4.

5.

The SeattleCoach Philosophical Foundations

The four-fold and pragmatic foundations
of the SeattleCoach approach

I think midlife is when the universe gently places her hands upon your shoulders, pulls you close, and whispers in your ear: "I'm not screwing around. It's time." —Brené Brown

When God wants to show you something, [God] takes you on a journey. —Bruce Larson

From the beginning of SeattleCoach in 2008, I've aimed for far more than training coaches. Believing that professional coaching is a twenty-first-century leadership movement, I've designed our work to deepen the personal style and presence, along with the coaching mindset, of each of our coaches. Our work of teaching our coaches and coaching leaders both the skills and personal presence of this craft is enriched by the following foundational components:

1. Psychological Competencies

Before I became a coach, I practiced for years as a licensed marriage and family therapist and became increasingly interested in the overlap of my work with the field of Industrial and Organizational Psychology. In our curriculum you will spot elements of Solution-Focused Brief Therapy, Acceptance and Commitment Therapy (ACT), Emotionally Focused Couples Therapy, Internal Family Systems, Motivational Interviewing, and Appreciative Inquiry.

2. Systems Theory

*Above all, you will experience my convictions about Systems Theory and its most foundational component—the leader and his or her personal presence. Good leadership is less about skill, data, or command-and-control of subject matter expertise and far more about the leader's ability to understand and navigate the relational climate of their family, group, or team. And in Systems Theory, this is referred to as **differentiated** leadership.*

A differentiated leader is marked by their calm personal authority, their openness to learning more about themselves and their impact, and their ability to then apply that wisdom in the moment. These are the leaders who can address reality curiously—resiliently anchored in their own lives—without slipping into automatic reactivity and blame. They listen to understand as readily as they listen to respond. Or as our coaches at Microsoft are fond of saying, they know how to "press pause, zoom out, and make a choice."

Differentiated leaders may not be the positional leader, but they are almost always the most influential. They are the leaders who know how to be both separate, and, at the same time, generously connected. They tend to be contagious in the best of ways, and that increases the overall quality and quantity of connections in the family, group, or team.

3. Applied Neuroscience

The third component is the emerging field of applied neuroscience—strengths-based/somatic intelligence and process. Simply put, our human brains learn best and change most positively and sustainably when we are in neurologically safe-enough alliances. "Safe-enough" does not mean bubble-wrapped. Coachable people are not delicate, insistent, entitled, or victimy. "Safe-enough" means that where there is enough predictability, autonomy, trust, compassion, and mutual respect, brains and relationships do better, especially in collaboration and conflict.

4. The Wisdom of the Seasoned Leaders We Attract

And finally, we trust the wise and eclectic human filters of the seasoned leaders we attract. We pick learners: people who are curious, brave, inclusive, and patient with discomfort. They don't scare easily. Our participant-coaches bring rich backgrounds in a variety of leadership and management approaches. And they apply their learning in a wide array of settings—with executives and teams, as in-house experts and HR professionals, and as external entrepreneurs who specialize in executive, individual, team, wellness, adventure, and personal development coaching. Because coaching often connects with one's sense of purpose, many of our coaches are informed by their personal faith backgrounds in Jewish, Buddhist, and Christian spiritualties.

In everything we do in the development of coaches and coaching leaders, we are highly personalized and face-to-face (both virtually and in-person). We have designed SeattleCoach to be a coach training and development program that leaves a community of support and collaboration in its wake.

*Finally, you are joining **a network of hundreds of other SeattleCoaches**[c] who share your coaching heart, approach, and vocabulary. On the resources page you'll find ways to connect with our larger trib.,*

1. *We keep all the latest news posted on our **SeattleCoach Network Group on LinkedIn.**[d]*

2. *You'll find additional articles, videos, and interviews, along with the link to sign up for our Substack newsletter, **"Coachable!"** right here.[e]*

3. *And every year we add faces to **our latest anniversary video**.[f]*

Working with Your Peer Coaches

If you are joining a "SeattleCoach Cohort" of fellow coaching leaders, think of your CFL experience as having three essential components.

First are our live general sessions, second is the independent study (reading, videos) we'll send before and following each session.

And third is the time you will spend coaching with other participants. This is where so much of the magic happens.

As you know, we choose our participants by asking ourselves, *"Would we want to be coached by this person?"* Happily, that has meant that SeattleCoaches come with the stuff that's hard to teach. When peer coaches like that train and practice together, they become significant allies, maybe even life-long friends.

So, here's our request: bring your own coachable self and your own coachable agenda to the members of your Cohort. You'll get some excellent coaching. And this, along with your personal reflection, will likely be transformative.

Between each of our sessions we'll ask you to meet with two or three of your peer coaches. Whether face-to-face, virtually, or on the phone (we want you to get good at each), everyone will have multiple opportunities to be the "coach," the "coachee," and the observer.

A note about giving and receiving "feedback-ish"

We know. Whether you are on the giving or the receiving end, that word, **feedback**, can be paralyzing. As in, *"I have some feedback for you. You'd better sit down."* Maybe (like with another word, **accountability**) you have a sad history with it.

At SeattleCoach we're on a mission to rehabilitate the word "feedback." We'll have much more to say about that later in our journey. We will be talking a lot about how coaches—with trust, compassion, and permission—speak truth, even hard truth, as they faithfully serve the people they lead and coach.

As we move through our months together, we think you will experience a little resetting as you give and receive the elements of great feedback **that comes from someone you trust**:

1. You speak from calm authority, using yourself and being open to learning and being influenced.
2. You seek to serve more than to please, to invite and to co-create rather than to confront.
3. When you catch someone being brilliant, you smile and mark the moment.
4. You are most interested in what the person you're listening to just said or did. It's almost always more fruitful if you get curious about *"What else? Can you say more about your thinking?"* than to respond right away with offers/invitations for them to think about something more or different or corrective from your own point of view.
5. You speak as closely as possible to the "event" or observation.
6. And you speak with curiosity and specifics—to what is strong or changeable and growing.

7. Over time, your feedback—and the relationship that fuels it—focuses on strengths, values, and accomplishments more than on failure and rough patches. We'll talk about the research behind an actual "feedback ratio" of 4:1 over time.

8. You stay mindful that the person you're listening to longs to be a great coach and that their version of "excellent" will be a little bit idiosyncratic.

9. And, of course, even when you're speaking with directness as a faithful "truth-teller," unless the house is on fire you are curious, respectful, and unhurried.

SeattleCoaches from several European countries have consistently observed, *"You Americans are so nice, and it's confusing! We're blunt and direct, and it's ok if you are too. Say what you mean!"* This is known as valuable feedback about giving feedback.

People hear us differently when they are safe enough to be open. Extend grace to your partners. You'll be practicing and coaching a lot with them. Your confidence will grow, and these peer coaches will likely become your trusted allies and friends. We'll have more to say about offering feedback as we grow together.

And two things you should know about how we like to start each of our times together

1. You can expect us to start and end on time. That's our agreement, and agreements are a big deal with coaches and coaching leaders.

2. And as we get underway in each session, we'll take a couple of minutes as a Cohort to "reset." We're all busy people, and we can be a little like Kramer from Seinfeld, skidding in sideways, coming in hot at the last minute. For a coach or coaching leader, resetting is simply the idea of doing what you need to do to become present with the rest of us. So see if you can build in a couple of minutes before we begin to take a breath. Then, in our first few sessions, we'll experiment for a few minutes with some of the elements of "resetting."

The Play Cards

Below are two SeattleCoach Play Cards:

1. One with ideas for your peer coaching conversations;

2. One with our thoughts about the "how" and "what" rhythm of any good coaching conversation.

We'll reference each one a lot. You may find it useful to make copies.

Working with Your Peer Coaches

I never fail. I either win or learn. —Nelson Mandela

Preparing for your meeting . . .

- **Everyone:** review your notes, readings from the **Playbook**, and your Play Card. What are the skills you want to explore, practice, and make your own?
- **Preparing to be the coach:** review your strengths, growing edges, and something you want to experiment with or get better at.
- **Preparing to be the coachee:** come prepared with a personal coachable agenda to practice with.

If you get stuck for an agenda, ask yourself, *What's coming up this week? An opportunity? An obstacle? Something to think through or get better at?* The most easily accessible coachable issues are often related to challenges you will face between now and the next conversation. For example: *a transition, a performance issue, a relationship challenge, an outcome, or maybe a communication strategy*.

When you're together . . .

1. Begin by establishing roles: choose a **coach**, a **coachee**, and an **observer**.
2. Decide who will watch the clock.
3. The **coach** sets the stage for good feedback by naming their **growing edge**.

Then for 20 minutes . . .

1. The **coach** and **coachee** work together exploring the agenda, what the evidence of success would be, why it matters, and maybe who else is in their thinking as they explore it. Find a next step.
2. **Observers** keep your focus on the coach and what the coach is doing.
3. After **20 minutes** of coaching, the coach and coachee agree on a good place to stop.

Coaches—when you're stuck, call a timeout to brainstorm with your triad for one minute.

Then for 10 minutes . . .

1. **Observers:** Be the "container" and guide the process.
2. **Start with the coachee:** *What worked? What are you more aware of? What would you have liked more of? Less of? What is unique about this coach? What will you do because of this conversation?*
3. **Then turn to the coach**: *What choices did you make? What did you experiment with? What did you notice about your internal dialog? What did you learn?*
4. **Finally, the observers:** *What did you notice about the growing edge that the coach identified? What did the coach do that got your attention?*

Then rotate roles and try again. In your weeks together, make sure everyone gets to "sit in each seat."

The Coaching Mindset: The "How"

**It is the personal presence of the coach or coaching leader that is the game-changer.
We call the following practices *"The Core Four."* Each practice fosters *The Coaching Mindset*.
And each practice may call for slowing your pace—just a little.**

Respect — *Coaches express respect for others' goals, agenda, opinions, confidences and resourcefulness.*
  ✓ Ask questions. Ask permission. Listen for the *"I-coulds."* Be patient with discomfort.

Energy — *Coaches study and use their personal energy, judgment, values, experience and intuition.*
  ✓ Understand the deep influence of your own voice, mood, breath and posture. The more you know, the more chosen (instead of reactive) you can be as you manage, lead and influence.

Acknowledgment — *Coaches acknowledge the admirable. saying what they see in the character, actions, strengths, self-responsibility and vision of others. Their words are genuine and clear, marked by both grace (support) and truth (directness and challenge).*
  ✓ The most useful acknowledgment/feedback/perspective is delivered authentically, specifically, respectfully and close to the event. It speaks to what is changeable and growing.

Listening — *When a strong coach listens well—usually beyond the actual words—they inspire clarity, energy and possibility. They evoke awareness. We call this "level 3" listening. You are listening for the most useful questions to ask vs. simply keeping a list of great questions.*
  ✓ Listening well matters even more than the amount of time spent. And, along with clarity and energy, it even may inspire deeper levels of intelligence, courage and self-efficacy.

In the SeattleCoach Stash: There's a video story about listening at Level 3.[g]

The Coaching Mindset: The "What"

**As a coach or coaching leader, you build on an alliance of trust, on clear agreements and on clarity about the purpose of the conversation--the agenda.
Your personal presence inspires the rhythm of exploration/experimentation.**

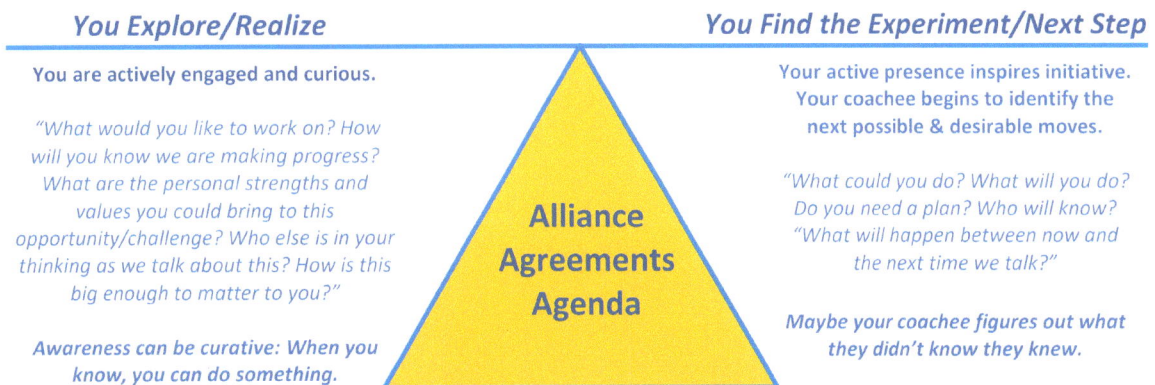

You Explore/Realize | *You Find the Experiment/Next Step*

You are actively engaged and curious.

"What would you like to work on? How will you know we are making progress? What are the personal strengths and values you could bring to this opportunity/challenge? Who else is in your thinking as we talk about this? How is this big enough to matter to you?"

Awareness can be curative: When you know, you can do something.

Alliance Agreements Agenda

Your active presence inspires initiative. Your coachee begins to identify the next possible & desirable moves.

"What could you do? What will you do? Do you need a plan? Who will know? "What will happen between now and the next time we talk?"

Maybe your coachee figures out what they didn't know they knew.

**Your coachee leaves the conversation with a next step.
Maybe their next step is to reflect—maybe it is to make a bold move.**

Doing the Craft, Part 1

Coachability and Human Change

Becoming Coachable

As coaches, we begin with the belief that the people we coach are creative, resourceful, and responsible for their own growth and change. They are ready to discover new things about themselves. That belief, of course, must begin with the way we approach our own lives—and our participation in SeattleCoach. With your peer coaches, you'll have a chance to explore your own defaults and habits and what it could look like to find your own possible and desirable next steps toward more contribution and satisfaction. You'll be challenged to be bravely vulnerable as trust grows. And you'll acquire a deep understanding of what we mean by "coachable."

All of us have spent time in each of the following "quadrants." People in each starting place either are or could become coachable if they are willing to look at their own insight and initiative. Can they be open to their own heart and hunches? Open to what makes them a gift to be around? Open to knowing what makes them annoying? Can they be tough-minded about taking responsibility rather than searching for someone to blame? Some arrive coachable. Others, with the right questions and expectations from you, may readily become coachable.

As you begin to coach others, you help them understand how coaching works. Remember? If you're a leader who wears several hats, there are urgent moments when your job is teach, fix, direct, manage, and deploy your subject matter expertise directly.

However, if your goal is to foster learning, performance, and improved competency and presence in individuals and teams over time, the challenge is to try the coaching gear first. Maybe the person you're talking to will join you. For example, the career discussion . . .

Classic opening line: *"Can you just tell me what to do? Solve this for me? Fix it?"* The coach explores **resources:** • What's in your way? • What do you feel confident about? • Where do you anticipate needing my help? • Who else do you think might have the skills/resources to help?	Classic opening line: *"It's time. I think I'm ready for the next challenge in my career."* The coach explores **what's possible & desirable:** • How do you know it's time? • What are you starting to think about? • What are you beginning to be ready for? • How hard are you willing to work? • Can you share a mental image of what this might look like? • If our coaching really worked . . .?
Classic opening line: *"So, this is supposed to be a career development discussion. Whatcha got for me?"* Or, *"So, I need to work on my collaboration skills in order to get to the next level? Ok, fine."* Or, *"My boss says I need a coach. She'll pay."* The coach explores **initiative:** • What benefit do you see in exploring this with me? • What if things stay the same?	Classic opening line: *"Making a change has been on my mind for a while, and I know it's important. But I'm mostly happy where I am now. I just don't know how I'd approach it."* The coach explores **pros and cons:** • What do you love about your current role? • What are some things you'd like to change? To keep? To leave behind? • What do you want to get better at? • How does that fit relative to what you're doing now?

Readiness for personal initiative/a next step (vertical axis)

(Low)

Readiness for personal insight (horizontal axis)

So, what if it turns out that the person you're coaching needs a different kind of resource instead of—or in addition to—their work with you?

Maybe the person you're in conversation with truly has a missing resource: They need direction, some specific legal or professional expertise, or maybe an executive decision. They may still be a coachable person with a coachable agenda, but they might also need someone else on their team. Through the years I have coached people who also work with therapists, lawyers, members of the clergy, and physical trainers and yoga teachers. Sometimes great coaching makes it possible for our coachees to address old injuries and stuck places of all kinds. Maybe they can do that as they continue their work with you. Maybe the two of you will push the pause button.

Either way, great coaches build a resource and referral network.

So, what will you do when that place in your gut starts flashing its yellow warning light?

- *When someone believes the location of change is exclusively outside of themselves and their focus is fixed on a grievance or entitlement or on the identity of being a victim; or*
- *When you see marked changes in mood or performance, withdrawal, or change in appearance;*
- *When you hear hopelessness (always at the core of suicidal thoughts);*
- *When a person is behaving unreasonably or unethically (or illegally); or*
- *If they are in active addiction or have a compelling mental health challenge; and/or*
- *If they are unable to look at ways in which they may be causing harm to other people.*

As a coach, I count on growth and healing. And referring someone to a therapist always required gentleness, directness, and clarity about my own professional boundaries. Following some very clear and gracious conversations through the years—times when I've turned people down for coaching or redirected them to another resource and explained why—I've seen people become unstuck in meaningful ways. And then sometimes I coach them again.

One of our SeattleCoach Faculty members, La Tasha Byers, ACC, has suggested this way of thinking about what's coachable and what's not:

Coaching sweet spots
- Navigating career aspirations and professional growth
- Exploring strengths and opportunities
- Processing and taking action on feedback
- Working through obstacles and potential derailers
- Experiencing coaching with team members

Seek support/guidance Get someone else "on the team"
- Severe and continued performance issues
- Purposeful discrimination or unethical behavior
- Threats of violence/harassment
- An enduring experience of grief and loss
- Unusual and frequent expressions of burnout, anger, and sadness
- When extremely time-sensitive decisions need to be made
- When a specific skill, data, or resource is needed

In the SeattleCoach Stash PDF: *Read more about referring a client to therapy, in an article from the International Coaching Federation (ICF).*[3]

Inviting Coaching Conversations

The word will get out that you're going through "Coaching for Leaders," and volunteers will start to appear. We'll help you find ways to recognize coachable moments, coachable agenda, and coachable people. Then we'll explore what it could be like to try coaching first (vs. telling, directing, advising, correcting, nagging, selling, convincing, propping up, rescuing, firefighting, etc.).

We also know that there are times when you as a leader simply need to give direction or to use your subject matter expertise. Sometimes the purpose of the conversation is time sensitive. Even in those settings, however, you will begin to recognize coachable moments with your colleagues, groups, and teams.

Many CFL leaders get underway by inviting their current mentees to experiment with coaching. Others simply explain that they're in CFL and then begin to infuse a coach-approach into their team meetings and scheduled one-on-one conversations. Regardless of how you test drive what we talk about, you may find that you have a huge impact in a very brief amount of time.

Bottom line, during training we want you to coach. A lot. Seriously. Listen, create safety and respect, work on insight-creation, and co-create the experiments that your coachees are ready for. And then ask your coachees for their feedback.

Another question operates in the background as you begin to let people know you are developing as a coaching leader: How do you like to work?

For example:

- Do you want to carve out specific "coaching time" or to find ways to weave it into existing one-on-one's with mentees, employees, and peers? What length of time will work best for you? Twenty minutes? Forty-five?
- You may have heard of "managing by walking around." Maybe you'll try "coaching by walking around."
- Will you track progress? Or will this be your coachee's job?
- How can you imagine using your subject matter expertise (SME) as you coach?

Start now to keep track of your "terms" as a manager or leader. If they matter to you, they will find their way into how you talk about this addition to your leadership. And your personal clarity will contribute to your trustworthiness as you build alliances with your coachees, employees, mentees, and team members.

Think about how you talk about yourself when welcoming a new team member or kicking off a project with new stakeholders. How will you talk about your emerging coaching "gear" in your leadership engine?

In the SeattleCoach Stash: "Talking about This Thing You're Doing and Becoming."[h]

Gradually, Then Suddenly: How Coaching Works

There is a much-quoted moment from Ernest Hemingway's 1926 novel, *The Sun Also Rises*, in which a character explains how he went bankrupt: *"Two ways,"* he says. *"Gradually and then suddenly."*[4]

We have all experienced it. Physics calls it the *tipping point*. A Buddhist proverb says, *"When the student is ready, the teacher will appear."* Jesus talked about acquiring *"eyes to see and ears to hear."* Lillian Hellman wrote in her 1969 novel, *An Unfinished Woman*, *"Nothing, of course, begins at the time you think it did."*[5] My grandfather, George Randall, laughed about "the last straw."

If you are like me, *"suddenly"* can be a quiet dawning or a jarring moment of truth. *"Suddenly"* can happen in your own awareness, or, if you wait too long, it can slam into you from the outside. It can be an epiphany or a moment of dread, or just a quiet conviction that something must change. For example:

- *Gradually, I have taken on too much at work, and all of a sudden (a) I'm mad, or (b) things are imploding.*
- *Gradually, I have wanted to volunteer more, and, out of the blue, this non-profit comes looking for me.*
- *Gradually, I have put on weight, and all of a sudden my chest hurts.*
- *Gradually, what I really want to do more of in my work has come into focus.*

Recently I heard a common "gradually" from a new coachee: *"Gradually,"* he said, *"I've gotten restless in my work. I know I am capable of far more contribution and satisfaction. I've thought about hiring you for a while, and this is the right time."*

In the months that followed, I walked with him as he held steady, faced obstacles, and got overwhelmed. He wondered out loud, *"Am I doing this right?!"* We talked about how his tone of voice sounded as he talked to himself. In each conversation, I'd ask some version of, *"What do you want to work on, leave behind, do more of, do less of, or get better at?"* Sometimes I heard a hunch that was just forming. We found experiments. If the experiment was useful, then why?

He was brave. Especially as he looked deeply at his own forty-five-year-old life. He pointed out quietly that he'd been thinking about the fact that he was *"half-way through."*

I love working with people like him.

Here are some answers that have come in response from others in the beginning of coaching relationships as I've asked the *"What-do-you-want-to-work-on?"* question:

- *"I want to be more inspiring as a leader."*
- *"I need a new job—maybe find my life's work."*
- *"My leader just doesn't stop to listen to me—I feel disrespected (and not for the first time). I need to figure out my part in that."*
- *"I want to lead my team better—and to see them collaborate better too."*
- *"I'm a lawyer, but I don't want to practice law anymore."*
- *"I think I could become the next CEO."*
- *"It's time for me to write something."*
- *"I'm ready to find a life partner."*

- *"We're having a baby."*
- *"The last baby is leaving home."*
- *"I need to make more money without losing my soul."*

Sometimes people hear me talk about "the wilderness." This is that span of time that usually begins before a clear ending and lasts well into the new beginning. You don't know how long it will last. It goes something like this (the biblical story of Moses comes to mind): Not only do you have your own disoriented questions, you also get some from the people who depend on you: *"Where are we going?" "Are you sure you know the way?" "What was so bad about the old situation anyway?"* These people will appreciate extra patience and engagement from you. You may think there are more important things to talk about, but they don't. In the wilderness, I think, you make extra time to keep your followers (and those who love you) well-informed and close to you.

Because the wilderness is confusing, ambiguous, scary, and fluid, we are tempted to hurry through it. But it's often where many of the biggest breakthroughs and creative opportunities come into focus. It's not necessarily a horrible place. Like any hero on a quest (even a reluctant one), you will meet with resistance that must be understood, overcome, accepted, or danced with as the transformation becomes irresistible.

Like any hero in the wilderness, maybe you'll learn things about being resilient when your heart breaks a little. Maybe you'll learn to be patient, open, willing to repeatedly test and learn, and, through it all, to listen to your life and strengths and values—and to the people closest to you. You will do hard things.

You can tell when you are getting close to "the beginning of the end" of the wilderness when your new direction begins to look like the new normal. You are determined, open, seeking, continuing to make small choices and you begin to perceive the right direction. You already know that any path through a wilderness is rarely straight and uncomplicated. Relapses, returns to the safety of what you wanted to leave, second thoughts, discouragement, and "squishiness" still happen, but they begin to diminish.

In this phase too, I continue to listen deeply, challenging and supporting. By now we'll have built trust, and I might become extra direct with a question or with a hard truth. And I'll acknowledge the character and strengths and values I see.

I know from my own experience that this level of courageous growth and sustainable change will affect your life in every way—spiritually, emotionally, physically, socially, and in the way you savor your days and relationships. The people I work with tend to keep it going, both as they work with me over time and as they find and grow their own coaching voice—the one that will stay with them after we've wrapped up our season of coaching together.

In the SeattleCoach Stash PDF*: Read more about coaching change in a book co-written by one of my favorite authors, Richard Boyatzis.[6] Or listen to an excellent Institute of Coaching interview with Boyatzis on effective coaching at https://www.instituteofcoaching.org/resources/webinar-grand-challenge-future-coaching.*

Exploratory Conversations

People change when they hurt enough that they have to, learn enough that they want to,
and receive enough that they are able to. —John C. Maxwell

It doesn't take long for the word to get out that you are learning to coach. Maybe your first coachee will be someone you're currently mentoring. When someone gets curious about coaching, they've usually formed a few questions and requests. And they also come with some restlessness, frustration, hope, and/or pain.

In my response to a new potential coachee, I usually say something like, *"Let's find a time to ask each other questions for about twenty minutes, and then I'll push the pause button and check in with you. I'll be most curious about your aspirations in coaching. If I think I can help, I'll tell you. If I think someone else, or another resource, would be a better fit, I'll tell you. If green lights ensue for both of us, then we'll keep talking."*

As we talk, I keep in mind my "coachability" questions and my own "how-do-you-like-to-work" questions. I ask them if it would be ok if I take a few notes.

This is the necessary conversation that happens on the way to co-creating the alliance, agreement, and agenda for good work together. Or not. **Let people experience you as a coaching leader right from the start. Show them what coaching is like. The type of coaching I am challenging you to get good at in the weeks and months to come is far more like an elegant conversation about your coachee's vision, restlessness, and aspirations than about their presenting problems, the application of a technique, or a magic formula of questions.** As you move through the conversation, if you find you're a match, great. If not, someone (maybe you) has been protected from a bad or mediocre experience.

For the first several minutes listen-listen-listen. Starting right here, you are connecting and becoming attuned. Remember, **Level 1** listening is for your own self-interest—maybe you're listening for something you need, or for an opportunity to respond, or to demonstrate your expertise. At **Level 2**, you're listening for data, information, context, history. A little bit of Level 2 can be useful, but a little goes a long way. It is at **Level 3** where the magic happens: you're listening—beyond the words—to understand the thinking, strengths, hopes, obstacles, and ways of this person before you.

You are creating the conditions of trust that are required for a different kind of conversation. Get a glimpse of your coachee's life, follow their energy, and find out about the thing that they want to solve or change or get better at. Invite them to deepen their experience of the reality of the potential shift. What if the shift happens? What if it doesn't? Reassurance ("Everything will probably work out . . .") isn't very useful here. As always, resist the impulse to solve problems, prop up, rescue, and fix things. This person has already (usually) tried most of what you might suggest anyway. They have likely reached out to you because they are at a point of transformational change: a major exploration, a letting-go, or maybe a crucial series of experiments and conversations.

1. Some potential questions:

    - *"What are you hoping for?"* (Sometimes the answer to this question takes some patient exploring.)
    - *"What have you tried? Where have you been stuck? What hurts?"*
    - *"What are you asking of yourself at this point in your life?"*
    - *"What are the personal strengths and values that you and I will be talking about?"*

- *"If you could do an internet search about what has your attention, what would you enter?"*
- *"What are the results you need? The behaviors that you think will be necessary? Challenges to anticipate?"*
- *"What will success look like?"* Explore goals specifically and behaviorally—their outcomes might surprise you. *("I'd contribute more. There'd be more trust on my team. I'd sleep better. Oh. And my teenager would talk to me again.")*
- *"Who and what does your work serve?"*
- *"Who's in your corner? How does your manager or significant other feel about what you want to work on in coaching? What about the investment of time and money?"*

Deepen the exploration: *"What if things stay as they are? What will success look like?"*
"Specifically, and behaviorally, what outcomes can you envision?"

2. Anticipate some of their questions and concerns about working with you.

- They are wondering, *Are you competent? Experienced? Trustworthy? Trained? What about confidentiality?*
- Anticipate logistical questions: *"How does coaching work? How long? How frequent?"*
- And a few bottom-line questions: *"Have you coached people like me before? Do you know what you're doing? Will there be the right blend of support and challenge?"*

This person is looking for a partner who will help them look at themselves and their situation with new eyes. Maybe they've come to the right place.

After a few minutes, check in: *"How is it for you as you talk to me about this?"*

3. Explain how you like to work: your calm clarity will be grounding. After all, you are building a trusted and priority relationship.

- *"Every time we meet, I'll begin by asking you what you'd like to work on. That will usually flow out of what's happened between our sessions."*
- *"Every time we meet, I'll hold your big picture—not just your focus—for the session of the day."*
- *"Every time we meet, we'll be paying attention to possible next steps."*
- *"From time to time, based on what we've explored, I'll have requests and challenges. When I do, I'll expect you to say yes or no, or to make me a counteroffer."*
- *"Here's how we might know we're at a stopping place . . ."*

4. Give your feedback and recommendations about possible next steps.

- *"Let me tell you what I've heard you say: You love, you hope, you're worried, the challenge for you is . . ."*
- *"This is a very coachable problem/issue/opportunity. I bet we'll do some good work together."*
- *"There might be a better resource for you."*

5. Some key things to pay attention to in yourself as you talk with a potential coachee:

- What's it like to be with this person? Any red flags in your intuition?
- Do you see any conflicts of interest? That is, dual relationships or a mission at odds with your own values?
- Will you be able to show up as an important part of this person's life confidently and consistently?

6. Collaborate on a next step.

- Talk about how you'll structure your time together: frequency, amount of time for each meeting, how long, etc.
- If you have some getting-started questions, ask your potential coachee to reflect on them before your first/next meeting.
- If this person needs a referral to someone other than you, offer to help them connect with the right resource. (You will begin to build your own referral list, but if you get stuck, call me any time.)

A good informational/exploratory conversation is the first step to building a potentially life-changing alliance and agreement and to understanding your coachee's agenda. At the end of twenty minutes, if it feels like a match to me, I ask them if they would like to move forward. If so, I pause, smile, mark the moment, and we launch.

In the SeattleCoach Stash PDF: Read more about building alliance, agreement, and agenda by Patrick Lencioni, another of my favorite authors.[7]

Note: Mr. Lencioni doesn't know it, but I've made him an unofficial member of the SeattleCoach tribe. His philosophy reflects our own when it comes to working with and serving people.

Coaching the Person, Not the Problem

Following a recent offsite with a leader and her team of fifteen, I received the following note from one of her very thoughtful senior team members:

> *Hi Patty. I had a question that came up for me during your session today with our team. It's a tactical question related to the idea of coaching the person, not the problem.*
>
> *I really like that notion and also realize that I'm more frequently in a "just-solve/fix-the-problem" mode than a "coach-the-person" mode during my one-one meetings. I was wondering if you had a one-on-one guide suggestion to help with that. Below is my one-on-one template. As you can see—it is very business- and problem-focused and does not facilitate coaching the way another approach perhaps could.*
>
> *Current Focus Areas*
>
> - *Hot Topics*
> - *Asks of Me*
> - *Priorities and deliverables with changes/status updates*

In response, I surveyed a few of our CFL veterans. These were some of their ideas about adding coaching to one-one conversations (in no particular order):

> - *"What has to happen in your work and in your development (this quarter/month) in order for you to think of this as a successful period?"*
> - *"What is keeping you up at night?"*
> - *"What are your growing edges?"*
> - *"Who else is in your thinking as we talk today?"*
> - *"What is challenging you? Where do you feel stuck? What has surprised you? What are you learning? Any missing resources? Roadblocks?"*

I usually ask coachees to reflect on a few questions like these prior to our meeting. More about that comes later in the **Playbook**. When my wish is granted and they have a conversation with themselves before they have one with me, the conversation gets richer.

The following tool—The Wheel—is one of my favorites. It helps to keep me focused on the person.

Using the Wheel with the People You Coach

If you've had a solid informational/exploratory conversation with a potential coachee and then received a coaching agreement from them, you've established some critical bits of information:

1. *Are you and this person a match to work together?*
2. *Is the person coachable? (Or is it hard for them to stop wishing you'd just tell them what do to?)*
3. *And are you beginning to get an initial idea of your coachee's big agenda/coachable issues? What do you hear about their commitment and capacity to take it on?*

As you follow their energy, you'll understand how broad/specific their agenda (i.e., their coachable issue) is and how urgent it feels. You'll begin to understand where they are in the change process.

All of this will inform the starting point and direction of your first few conversations. You'll clarify and you'll prioritize, and, as trust grows, the agenda will evolve and deepen.

The tools below will help you build the habit of coaching the person, not the problem.

Below are examples of a **general Life-Flyover Wheel** and a **more specific Big-Agenda Wheel**. Depending on what I've heard in our informational/exploratory conversations, I'll send one or the other for my coachee to think about and write on prior to our next conversations.

Through the years, I've found that many people want to begin with an overview before homing in on the place of greatest interest or urgency in their personal or professional lives. When they do, usually a slice of the first Wheel is elevated to its own Wheel.

As I've mentioned, if you are a coaching leader in an organization, The Wheel may include things like the coachee's job description, the company's values and outcomes, or the supervisor's priorities. I may ask a sponsor to weigh in with a question like, "As this coachee and I work together over the coming months, what will be a trend in their performance and presence that will be important to you?" If, for example, you're working with a new people manager, the parts of The Wheel will usually include key expectations of the job, what the coachee wants to get better at, and what matters with the supervisor. Then the coaching begins with exploration about which first steps are most possible and desirable in the thinking of your coachee. You listen for how serious your coachee is about committing to those first steps.

As you move from general (usually a meta-agenda: *"I've been in this role for five years. I'm ready for a new challenge."*) to specific (*"I need to review finances with my spouse to see what's possible/desirable."*), continuing to listen for hopes and resources, people sometimes surprise themselves with what will help them create movement (like the man who wanted to move up in his company but decided that a first step related to his confidence. He decided to stop smoking).

Sometimes the people we coach start with the low-hanging fruit because, I think, accomplishment gives us humans a surge of energy for tackling bigger things. For example, through the years I have seen more than a few people leave their first sessions with a plan to simply create order in their physical environment, or to pay off a small credit card balance that has been bugging them. Low-hanging fruit = a good start that sets the stage for more.

The **Wheels** below will help you work with your coachee to explore starting points and the dimensions—and even incentives—of their challenges and opportunities. ***Note: Coaching the person is so much more fun than coaching the problem.***

In the SeattleCoach Stash: *Listen to my six minutes on using "The Wheel."* [i]

The Life-Flyover Wheel

Your Name: _____ Today's Date: _____

The sections of The Wheel provide a way of thinking about balance and satisfaction through the various parts of your life. Each slice is simply an area that matters to you, especially at this time in your life. In our first few sessions, we'll look at how satisfying (or unsatisfying) each one is to you at this point in your life.

Take a few minutes to label your own slices around the circumference of The Wheel. And please bring a copy to upcoming sessions. Some sample flyover slices (in no particular order):

- Your career and professional development and path: what are you ready to explore?
- Your current job description: what do you want to get better at?
- Your company or supervisor's priorities
- Building your friendships/support
- Finding a life partner
- Deepening your significant relationships: with your spouse, children, family of origin

- Health and fitness/spirituality
- Your physical environment and sense of order (home or work)
- Financial order
- Fun and play
- Your "true moral obligations"
- Giving back: an ability, gift, or passion to contribute (Leadership and organization? Inspiration? Hospitality? Time? $$?)

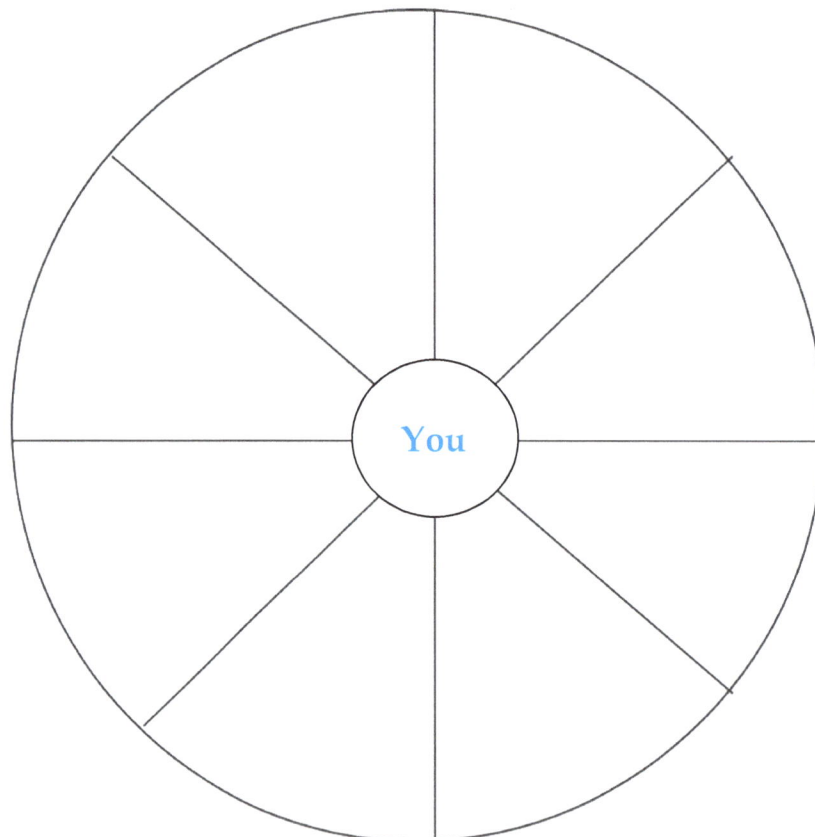

The Big-Agenda Wheel

Your Name: _____ Today's Date: _____

Most of the people you coach will show up with something specific in mind: a challenge, a project, a problem, or plans for their career development. They are ready—or beginning to be ready—to focus.

For example, people have brought some of these "hubs" to their informational/exploratory conversations: identifying and developing the capacities that are required for a new job; building a plan for a successful first-100 days in a new role; transitioning to or from something big, personally or professionally; maintaining pace and progress with a longitudinal, multi-dimensional project or assignment; or building a great team as a new team leader.

With the person I am coaching I get curious about the various dimensions of their "hub." As they identify their "slices," we get clear about strengths, priorities, obstacles, and key people. This is the conversation that will help the partnership refine the goals that are the most desirable and possible.

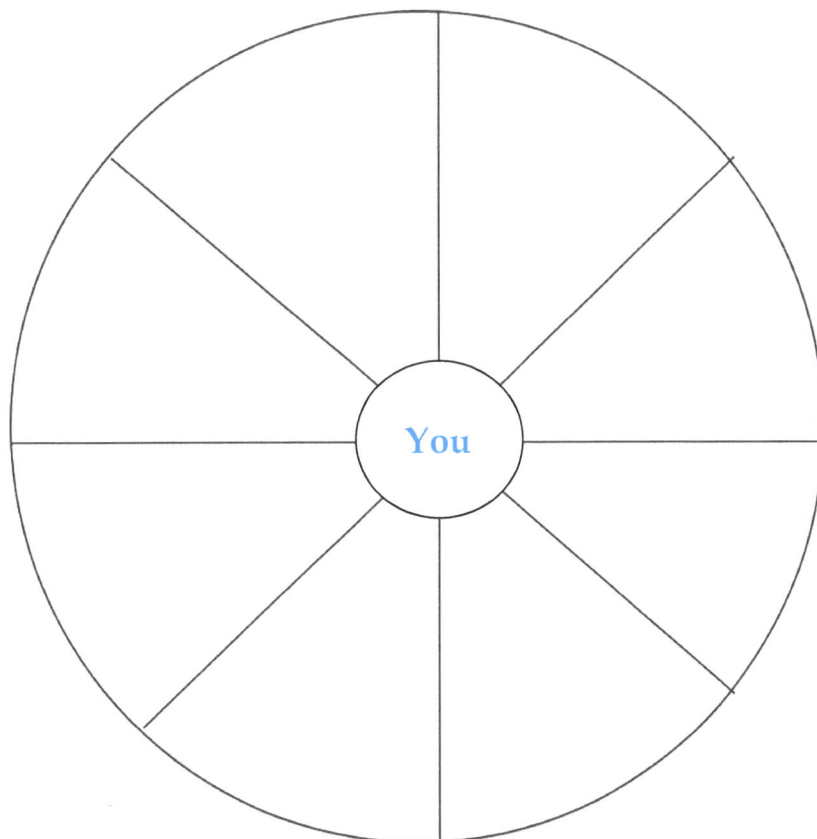

Coaching through Change

It's funny, isn't it? Our brains tend to hate change—and are very good at it. Coaches and coaching leaders are specialists in understanding and fostering positive human change. We make it easier, more possible. We help people identify and get over their stuckness, fear, and inadequacy. We help them move and grow through it. And when we recede into the background of their lives, we leave them with the beginnings of their own inner coach. We know that the world favors rapid learning, resilience, and collaboration. Our job is to make transitions easier, more thoughtful, sustainable, and even enjoyable and life-giving. Think of coaching as a way of delivering highly customized and interactive, just-in-time adult learning and leadership development.

As we have designed this course for internal coaching leaders, we have wrestled with a judgment call that each of you faces on a regular basis: when you and your team/direct reports are facing a big challenge, how will you coach them, and, as a coaching leader, how will you deliver your subject matter expertise and direction when it's needed? Thoughtful change management at its best develops good people, good products and services, and even good coaching cultures.

Sometimes when we ask "What do you want to work on?" the answer is in the category of "first-order change"; that is, something that the person you're coaching is already doing needs to change (more of? less of?). First-order change is always reversible. Sometimes what seems like a great idea is "just not right." If it is "not right," then why?

First-Order Change

We've been talking about change—and all of its alleged synonyms in the English language—from compliance to transformation. We talked about how in the lives of each of us there are times when we joyfully embrace change: it's our own choice and our own pace. And there are those other times when change crashes down upon us—times when we don't see it coming, or it just becomes unavoidable. Either way, we usually find ourselves in the wilderness.

What timber is to a logger, change is to us in our work as coaches and coaching leaders. We must understand its ways, its risks, its value, and how it behaves—and, as always, what the choices are. Even in the wilderness there are choices.

You already know how to listen at Level 2 and Level 3, and you already know how to build an alliance and use your own grace and wisdom in being compassionately curious. You already know how to listen for what's possible and desirable in the thinking of the person you're coaching given their stage of change.

Our work often applies to what is known as **"first-order change"**—that is, in the work of doing more, or less, of something we are already doing. First-order change may improve things significantly. And it's always reversible. This is the domain of "test and learn."

For example, a manager is restless and knows he needs more challenge, support, and development. He tells you, *"I like this company, but they don't see that I could add much more value from where I sit."* You reflect back, *"It sounds like you'd be happy to stay if a few things shifted, like if you approached the company with some of your ideas—and they liked them!"*

So maybe as you and this manager work together, you explore and find the right experiments and there's a happy ending both for the manager and his company. A lot of coaching happens with first-order change:

- You make adjustments to what is already mostly in place.
- New learning happens at a measured pace.
- The story is starting to feel new but in a comfort-zone kind of way.

And then there's "Second-Order Change"

Ivan Doig's wonderful novel ***Dancing at the Rascal Fair***[8] tells the story of two young Scottish immigrants who come to Montana in the late nineteenth century. Doig quotes from *Crawford's Transatlantic Emigrant's Guide,* one of the many books written at that time with advice for potential European and British emigrants. Here's an excerpt:

> *Do not emigrate in a fever but consider the question in each and every aspect. The Mother country must be left behind, the family ties, all old associations, broken. Be sure that you look at the dark side of the picture: the broad Atlantic, the dusty ride to the great West of America, the scorching sun, the cold winter—coldest ever you experienced!—and the hard work of the homestead. But if you finally, with your eyes open, decide to emigrate, do it nobly. Do it with no divided heart. . . .*
>
> *. . . We find, from our experience, that the mid-point of the journey is its lowest mark, mentally speaking. If doubt should afflict you thereabout, remonstrate with yourself that of the halves of your great voyage, the emigration part has been passed through, the immigration portion has now begun.*

Second-order change is deciding, or being forced to decide, to do something fundamentally different from what you've done before in your life. And, like the decision of these young Scots to emigrate, the change is irreversible. Once you've begun, it's not possible to ever return to the way things were. And the dimensions of the change can be emotionally overwhelming: changes in finances, in the expectations and judgments of others, even in your sense of yourself.

Second-order change is disruptive and potentially innovative. Maybe your calculated risk will fundamentally change a process or a market—or you, changing the rules while everyone else continues to march in a traditional direction. How will you even begin to think about this? First to yourself, then to allies, then to the world?

Right about here, one of your own second-order-change stories probably comes to mind. What did that chapter of your life require of you? How did the stages of change apply?

These are some of the brave people I've coached who come to mind:

- The long-time incumbent who lost his election.
- The guy who was tapped to become the new director of his own team.
- The coachee who got sober.
- The woman whose husband became a quadriplegic in a skiing accident.
- The Roman Catholic priest who thoughtfully concluded that his path was to become a husband and father. (No, he hadn't yet met the inspiring woman who would be his wife. He just knew.)
- The woman who decided at 35 to come out.
- The coachee who asked if he could bring his fiancée to his upcoming conversations with me.

If you'd have been the coach for any of these great people, can you imagine how you'd have helped him or her to "pull apart" the complexity of their change? Each one knew at some level that they were moving into a wilderness and that "going back" wasn't an option.

When you're coaching **second-order change**:

- New ways of seeing possibilities in life are beginning to emerge.
- As a safe presence, you may be the first to hear the news. (You'll be on sacred ground.)
- The person you're coaching is going through a fundamental transformation. There are scores of dimensions and implications.
- There will almost certainly be a period of wilderness for the coaching partnership to move through together. You will ask lots of questions to which you don't yet have answers.

When you are coaching second-order change, you spend significant time in emotional rehearsal, helping your coachee "try on" what they will say and how they will talk about the change. And to whom. And when.

Whether the person you're coaching is addressing improved performance or considering a game-changer, as a serious coach you're working closely with the inner process of a sacred human life.

Think about a time when you experienced second-order change. Maybe it was voluntary, maybe not. Maybe it was wonderful. Maybe it was terrible. Either way, you knew it was big, you knew it was a one-way door. In time you may have had a profound sense of grace and acceptance. Many people report that they pray during times of second-order change. When you think about your own experience of quantum change, how could a coaching leader have helped?

There are many "change models" out there that focus on the problem, the process, or the organization. We focus on the person—their hopes, stuck places, resources, opportunities, and desired outcomes.

The following two change models will help you think about how, with a coaching mindset, we humans can change our brains and lives in ways that are powerful, deliberate, and sustainable.

_____

In the SeattleCoach Stash PDF*: See three authors who have helped me to think about how we navigate change: Gregory Bateson, William H. Bergquist, and William Bridges.*[9]

Change Model #1: Finding Fun & Flow

Flow (that NE corner) is the dynamic True North of coachable people. Remember? They're open to reflect + open to try stuff. In Flow you learn to recognize the right challenges and to go after them with a trip to the NW corner. In Flow you also recognize when you need time to consolidate what you've learned with a sojourn into the SE corner: Maybe for a season, maybe for a brief reset.

Think of Flow, in the life of a professional coach or coaching leader, as the practice of listening steadily to your own life. Because the most important thing is what you do next.

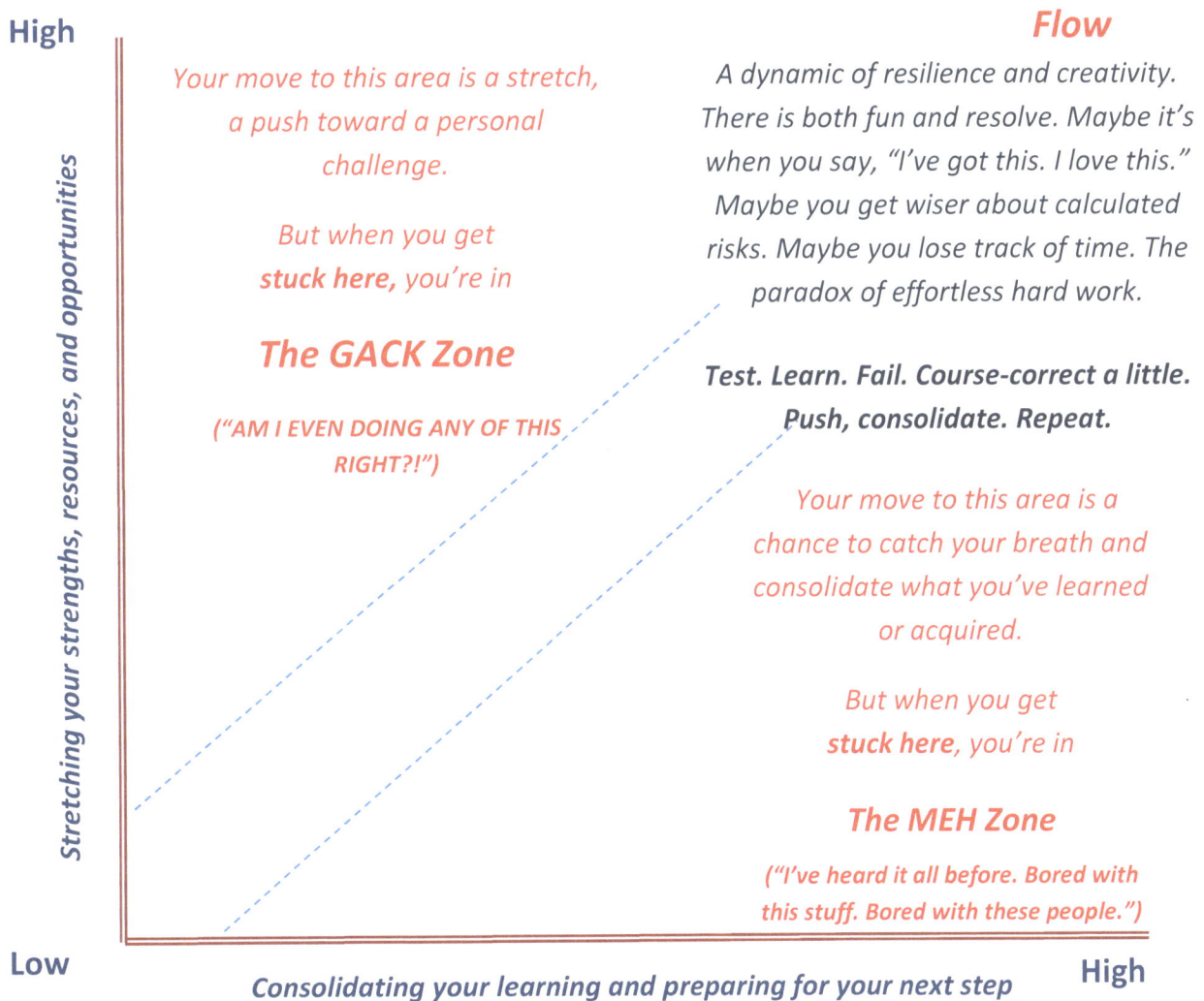

High

Stretching your strengths, resources, and opportunities

Your move to this area is a stretch, a push toward a personal challenge.

*But when you get **stuck here,** you're in*

The GACK Zone

("AM I EVEN DOING ANY OF THIS RIGHT?!")

Flow

A dynamic of resilience and creativity. There is both fun and resolve. Maybe it's when you say, "I've got this. I love this." Maybe you get wiser about calculated risks. Maybe you lose track of time. The paradox of effortless hard work.

Test. Learn. Fail. Course-correct a little. Push, consolidate. Repeat.

Your move to this area is a chance to catch your breath and consolidate what you've learned or acquired.

*But when you get **stuck here**, you're in*

The MEH Zone

("I've heard it all before. Bored with this stuff. Bored with these people.")

Low   *Consolidating your learning and preparing for your next step*   **High**

In the SeattleCoach Stash: Listen to my three minutes about "Finding Flow." **And in the SeattleCoach Stash PDF**: *Read more from* **Mihaly Csikszentmihalyi,** *the guy who started the "Flow" conversation.*[10]

Change Model #2: The Transtheoretical Model

This second model of how human brains successfully approach and metabolize change is based on the idea that we all work hard to keep ourselves in a safe-enough state of **flow**. This means that when we have a say in the matter, we move through a series of stages and stories when we are changing our behavior or our lives.

Think about a big change you've moved through: Becoming a new leader? Getting married? Becoming a parent? Recovering from a break-up or an addiction, or coming out in some way, or learning to live in a new country or culture? Grieving the loss of someone dear to you? Changing the path of your career? Whatever the change was, it took a while, didn't it? It was far more than analyzing data points. Your heart, your emotion led the way.

Change tends to begin with a story we're telling ourselves. Our attention to story is built into the very architecture of our brains. Stories help us—even more than data, at least at the start of the process—to make sense of things. So, when coaches and their coachees, at each of the following stages, get curious about story and tone and self-talk, their alliance deepens. *"What is possible? What is desirable? What are you ready for?"* Is it time for more safety and support and contemplation? Or more challenge and truth and action?

How quickly do people move through the stages of deep change? It varies, of course, but if there is a great coach in the picture, the change might get deeper, wider, and more sustainable.

You know from using The Wheel that it is normal for people to hold several points of transition and growth at the same time. Often the "slices" are complementary. As you help your coachee focus on the area that is most fruitful and accessible, you will likely find them orbiting one of the following stages.

Below are the stages of change in James Prochaska's "Transtheoretical Model."[11] Following each stage are a few comments about markers I look for and some "Stage Appropriate" questions I ask.

Stage 1: Precontemplation

In precontemplation, you have not yet decided to make a change—or even to accept it. At this stage, you are not ready to **just do it**. You may even be resistant, demoralized, and underestimating the potential gifts of change. But you have this hunch that something compelling (and maybe a bit scary) is on your horizon.

You're thinking: *I don't know . . . I've tried . . . I don't see how . . . I don't need to . . . change is costly.*

Your coach is gently curious, rolling with resistance, and normalizing "recycling." *What's bringing this up for you? And why now? What if? **What are you saying to yourself, and how are you saying it? When you listen to your emotion, what's the story?*** There is an evolving balance between pros and cons.

Then, maybe gently, the pros begin to outweigh the cons, and you find yourself moving into . . .

Stage 2: Contemplation

Now you're seriously considering making a change, but you're not ready to do a big public roll-out. The story is changing, and with it, the pros and cons of change are pulling even. But there's still ambivalence. You're moving toward deciding, maybe intending to act in the coming days or weeks. Your next step is reflection and planning. If you move back to pre-contemplation, maybe that's to be respected. (This is the stage when a lot of people call on the services of a good coach or coaching leader.)

You're thinking: *Hmm. Maybe I need to . . . I met someone who's actually done this . . .* You're remembering stories, evaluating, compromising, expanding, contracting. Maybe you just want to process out loud with someone you respect.

Your coach asks questions like: *"What do you see when you play it out? And how does each side line up with your values? What would this require of you, your strengths, and resources? What are the obstacles? Is that door really closed? What if it is? Who else knows what you're contemplating? What are you saying to yourself, and how are you saying it? When you listen to your emotion, what's the story?"*

Note to coaches: When you're coaching someone who is in contemplation, the "experiment" you land on will likely be, well, contemplative: *"It sounds like you process things when on your walks (when you journal, pray, talk to your spouse . . .). Would you be willing to do that daily between now and the next time we see each other?"*

As your "slow hunch" grows toward certainty, your story starts to change.

You begin to imagine or consider . . .

Stage 3: Determination/Preparation

In determination/preparation, the balance between the cons and the pros has tipped toward the pros. Your heart is informing your pros and cons. You're planning to act soon. Maybe even to share your big idea with more trusted allies, friends, and family.

You're thinking: *OK. I need to consider how I'll do this. It's time. I will. What could I do? Who will I tell first? What will I keep? What will I leave behind?* You're starting to be determined and willing, ready to take the first steps, to test and learn.

Your coach starts to ask about the potential specifics of your plan with questions like: *"What will you do? What do you need? Who will be in your corner? How will you know when you are ready to take action? What needs to be tested? How will you set up your environment to be conducive to your next steps? What payoffs do you see now?"* As before, your coach asks, *"What are you saying to yourself, and how are you saying it? When you listen to your emotion, what's the story?"*

Stage 4: Action

Now it's time to start testing and learning. You already know this won't be a simple roll-out or straight line. Maybe you'll experience two worlds, two stories, for a while. You continue to build support and to refine your steps into the new one. This is likely a lengthy period of creating and sustaining the change you're ready for. It could be a whole new chapter.

You're thinking: *I'm starting to make changes. Why'd I wait so long? This is hard—will it be worth it?* You are active, reflective, brave, energized, and accepting.

Your coach engages with you with questions like: *"What needs to happen this week? What are you paying attention to? Hmm. That didn't work. What did you learn? What will you keep? Are you starting to say 'good-bye' to anything? What is there more room for?"* And, as always, *"What are you saying to yourself, and how are you saying it? When you listen to your emotion, what's the story?"*

Note: At this stage, it's not uncommon to "push the pause button" and re-evaluate if all this investment of time and energy is really worth it. How can you help your coachee to anticipate this part of the process? If a coachee really has moved through stages 1–3, but continues to tap the brakes, this may be when a coach with great signal strength becomes extra direct and challenging. In the words of one smiling coach to her coachee, *"If this is not a new story, are you going to stop talking about it?"*

Stage 5: Maintenance/Consolidation

It begins to occur to you that you're sustaining a new skill or habit or story—a new addition—in your life. It's been a few months and you've realized you're doing this. The pros are obvious at every level.

You're thinking, *Wow. A new chapter. I don't want to let this go. I want to keep working and building.* You're feeling accomplished, steadfast, and optimistic. Speed bumps don't throw you off.

Your coach works with you on the speed bumps and helps you pay attention to your well-earned benefits: *"What are you noticing? What do you continually need to move out of your way? What do you love about this new normal? What's the story now?"*

Stage 6: Evaluation and then. . .? The pause button? A new challenge?

You've done it. You're steady with your new story. You're reminded of the strengths and values and relationships that mean the most to you. More of your story is yet to be written.

You're thinking, *I don't want to let this go; I know what to expect and how to be resilient with whatever comes.*

Your coach joins you in celebrating the character and behaviors this has required: *"What have you learned about how YOU create and sustain change? What are you contemplating now?"* And (as always), *"What are you saying to yourself, and how are you saying it?"*

And the cycle continues. It's no surprise that this is rarely a straight-line process for human brains. And, like our coachees, we're usually testing-and-learning through the stages of our own changes. Can you be steady and gentle, supportive, and challenging in both directions?

In other words, be prepared to normalize returns to earlier stages, and maybe for growth into new and unexpected directions as the possibility of change opens up. Our job as coaches is to recognize, accept, and continue creating engagement and safety for both hearts and brains.

Maybe you've noticed that in addition to talking about Prochaska's stages, I've also talked about the stories we tell ourselves as we move through the chapters of our lives.

When telling your story begins to feel important, you may find it useful to listen to the recording by Lisa Cron, the author of *Story or Die* (see reference immediately below). I bet you'll like it as much as I do.

In the SeattleCoach Stash *PDF: See a few more books about coaching change.[12] And a video by Lisa Cron about telling one of your personal change stories. I bet you'll like it as much as I do.[13]*

Maintaining Pace and Focus

At each step of the way with the people we coach—from the informational/exploratory conversation to The Wheel to an agreement—a big part of our job is to encourage our coachees' conversations with themselves, to keep a clear focus on their agenda and outcomes and on the pace of our work.

That's partly their job. But if I do my job well, the people I coach are learning to coach themselves between our conversations.

Sometimes people send me a quick note. Sometimes they use the questions below. Either way, I invite them into a reflective conversation with themselves before they come to the one with me.

The people I coach begin to anticipate what I might ask them about:

1. *"What would you like to work on?"* I listen for their best hopes and aspirations.
2. *"How will you know we are making progress? If we hit the nail on the head in the next 30 minutes, what would you have? If this conversation helps, what will shift? What will be clear that seems fuzzy now? How will you know when you have it?"*
3. *"What are the strengths and values you could bring to this opportunity/challenge?"*
4. *"Who else is in your thinking as we talk about this?"* (The answers may surprise you.)
5. *"How is this big enough to matter to you in the larger scheme of things (to your vision and values)?"*

Of course, life happens between conversations, but these questions invite both coachee and coach to take a moment to reflect and prepare. And when that happens, coaching conversations get more interesting and useful.

If my wish isn't granted and I don't receive something prior to our meeting, I simply take time at the beginning of the session to explore some of the same questions.

Doing the Craft, Part 2

Key Coaching Skills and Behaviors

Key Coaching Skills and Behaviors

Part 1/Co-creating a Level 3 Conversation

As coaches, in the way we listen—not only to content but also to another's voice, breath, tone, mood, nonverbals, and posture—we inspire a different kind of conversation. If **Level 1** conversation is transactional and **Level 2** is an exchange of points of view and data, **Level 3** is an unhurried co-creation. An alchemy. As coaches, we cultivate the ability to listen to our own lives; to the thoughts, emotions, and hunches of others; and to the larger systems of which we and they are part. With these skills, you "double-click" on the richest possibilities. Sometimes as we listen people who haven't recently been listened to much come back to life a little.

Saying what you see and hear. Every human has a way of saying, *"Don't miss this!"* Sometimes it's verbal. It always has nonverbal elements. Coaches listen beyond the words to the shifts right in front of them— for beliefs, energy, mood, behavior, voice, and posture. This doesn't mean you paraphrase, interpret, and diagnose. You simply notice: *"Your voice just got really soft." "You just teared up." "You just moved to the edge of your seat." "What just happened?" "What's going on in your thinking?" "I love what you just did!"* (Then, wait for it . . .) In the words of Alice Miller, *"You can listen like a blank wall or like a splendid auditorium where every sound comes back fuller and richer."*[14] What else is going on here? Saying what you see and hear may be the most connected and immediate way of giving useful feedback to your coachee. And it's not always easy. Sometimes it's a hard truth that no one else is brave enough to deliver: *"When you use that coarse language, I stop listening for a moment."* And as you say what you see and hear, you will likely inspire your coachee to listen with more grace and clarity to their own life. And when they do, their voice, and even their performance, will reflect it.

"Reset"/finding the focus. When you're hosting a special meal, you set the table with some care, and then, as everyone gathers around it, you do something to mark the moment. Maybe you propose a toast. Or say grace. Or maybe you simply smile at each of the faces looking at you as you begin and thank them for being present. Similarly, at the start of a coaching session, a good coach takes time to set the table for a safe and generative Level 3 conversation. I'll often ask my coachee to briefly *"take a moment and catch me up."* Or maybe I'll invite them to **"catch their breath"** (physically and emotionally) and "check in with themselves" as they finish arriving from a busy life. Then I'll ask, *"Where would you like to start?" ("Where we left off?" "That item from your focus form?" "Something else?")*

Clearing the deck. When a coachee shows up with some news about the results of a personal experiment, or something else immediate or emotional (maybe they're scared, disorganized, mad, or excited), or when there's something big in the news, what will you do? Maybe there's a lot going on "below the water line." Maybe a little longer neurological or somatic reset—or a release valve—is in order. When you "clear the deck," you patiently and supportively make some extra room: *"Would you take a breath, and then take five minutes to tell me what's happened? What is this like for you?"* At the end of five minutes, check in with your coachee: *"What do you think—do you want to return to/keep going on what we were working on? Does this thing on your mind need more attention?"* Sometimes the "clearing the deck" story changes the agenda you'd planned on, but usually that's your coachee's call.

Finding the right pace. As you set the stage for trust and success, you help the coachee articulate and manage their agenda, pace, the stage of change, and their markers of progress. In addition to your growing alliance and safety, tools like the informational/exploratory conversation, The Wheel, your written agreement/contract, and the Focus Form will help you co-create the right pace.

Clarifying focus. The coach's focus is not on being right; it's on finding the "thread" and being open to surprise, learning, not-knowing, correction, and co-creation. What is possible in your coachee's thinking? What is priority? What is urgent? What are they hoping for? Cultivate a learner's mind. Can you be OK with not-knowing? *"You sound ready to take this on. Did I get it?" "What would be different?" "What if you don't?"*

Meta-view. Expanding a perspective that has become cluttered or unclear. The meta-view can be a balcony, a time machine, or simply, *"Could we take a step back?"* (Find one you like to use.)

Metaphor. A good simile shoots off associations and learning like sparks. The best ones come from the people we coach and are like floodlights. We recognize how they rhyme. The coach just has to listen for them and then use them. One of my coachees, a novelist stuck in writer's block, said, *"It's like I'm trying to start a fire and I've got a big log but no kindling."* She inspired a great coaching conversation.

Time-out. I know, your mom told you not to, but this is a gracious (never-impatient) interruption. *"Could I stop you? Do you believe what you just said? It had the ring of truth."* With a time-out, you help your coachee wake up to the core of their story or to the moment in which they say or do something important or even exceptional.

Bottom line. Sometimes a coach calls a **time-out** to ask a key question: *"Can you give me the essence of what you are saying?"* I use this skill (again, never with impatience) when I begin to wonder how a coachee's long explanation is related to their agenda. (Or is it?) A coach I know challenges his coachees to *"stop talking and say something!"* Then again, maybe the story needs to be told.

Reframing. Let's say you're walking down the street and you pass a friend. Normally, your friend would greet you warmly, but today they don't even acknowledge you. What is the emotion you feel? Lots of options here: anxious, angry, sad, offended, surprised, curious? And what meaning do you attach to that emotion? What is the conclusion you draw? And then what do you do? It's easy for human brains to follow the **event-emotion-belief-action sequence.** Do you take a moment to explore the possibilities? Or do you act, maybe unhelpfully, on an unexamined emotion and belief, or maybe an old story that has nothing to do with your friend?

A good coach invites and makes time for examination and for potentially alternative conclusions and explanations (this includes **meta-view)**. Maybe we ask, *"What do you make of that? . . . What did you learn? . . . What will you do next?"* You remember that critical voices (See **Part 2** below) get busy with unexamined emotions, so you stay gently curious about that event-emotion-belief-action sequence: *"Is this about you? Is this always how it turns out for you? What was missing this time?"*

Sometimes the narrative (explanation) you or your coachee come up with isn't the truth. Sometimes the truth is just the hard, complicated truth.

Reframing doesn't mean you become a Pollyanna or that you fail to faithfully and bravely offer a hard truth (see **direct communication** below). As with many coaching skills, when you challenge your coachee to courageously reframe, it might become their skill too.

Level 3 questioning. The early nineteenth-century French novelist Honoré de Balzac is said to have stated: *"Power is revealed not by striking hard and often but by striking true."* This Key Skill is in RED because questions that are big enough to matter, and that are asked well, are at the heart of great coaching. Notice, it's not just "questions," it's **Level 3 questioning**. Your best questions as a coach don't come from a memorized list (though we all have a few favorites); rather, they are informed by the conversation itself and by the way you listen. Sometimes, like a great journalist, you just have to be brave and ask the obvious question *("Why did you do that if you thought it was wrong?")*.

Level 3 questioning deepens the coachee's awareness. The best questions are open-ended, direct, and to the point. Then be quiet and wait. Don't give up on your question while the person you are coaching is thinking, even wrestling with a new layer of awareness or with something they've avoided. Maybe ask again. Or ask, *"What else?"*

Level 3 questioning promotes discovery and isn't leading: *"What do you need to do to take care of yourself this week?"* (asked gently) is more useful than, *"Would it be helpful to take a day off?"* (which is really a bit of advice). Sometimes a great coaching artist sounds as curious and immediate as a fourth grader: *"How'd you do that?!"* Another great artist, Pablo Picasso, pointed out, *"It took me four years to paint like Raphael but a lifetime to paint like a child."*[15]

An inquiry is simply a transformational question offered (usually gently) or restated at the end of a session, for continued reflection: *"The big question I hear you contemplating today is, 'What if I don't do this?' Don't answer that right now. But would you notice your emerging hunches over the coming days? Could I ask you about that next time?"*

In the SeattleCoach Stash: *Listen to my four minutes about the "Gaze/Glance" rhythm of coaching conversations.*[k]

Key Coaching Skills and Behaviors

Part 2/Exploring Resistance

Five common reasons why humans tap the brakes.

Resistance is always full of information. When coaches learn to listen for it and then to explore it for meaning, the partnership deepens. Does the resistance come from inside? From outside? Is it true and useful? Is it false? Is the caution you hear helpful? Or is your coachee avoiding something important?

What old and potentially limiting stories, feelings, structures are in play? The coachee says, *"I've never been very organized. I am the youngest-born, after all."* Maybe you've found a growing edge to explore.

What resources are missing? Internally? Externally? What are your options when your coachee says, *"I want to apply for this job, but there's an item on the job description with which I've only got limited practice."* Sometimes we help people uncover what they didn't know they knew. But the answers aren't always "within." So sometimes we help our resourceful coachees to work on the best places to find the missing resource. If, as a coach, you are in true possession of the missing resource, you don't have to "hide the ball." It's fine to share that resource directly but without attachment to being right. And then to invite evaluation.

Where is this person on the change scale? 'What's happening with their balance of pros and cons? Maybe this is a useful caution. (The coachee: *"I'm just not ready to go public with this yet."*) What will your next question be?

What are his or her competing commitments—and resulting beliefs? In the evolution of the most successful cultures, we have lived with balances and trade-offs: grace vs. truth; rules vs. freedom; prosecute vs. dismiss; our personal rights, injuries, and longings vs. our need to belong, to find common ground, and to serve. It can be very easy, even automatic, for human brains to retreat to polarities where there are few shades of gray—and even less curiosity. True, sometimes there is a clear-cut answer to which you must bravely commit. But, more often, what if this is one of those generative and ongoing conversations with which you must stay patiently and graciously engaged with others over time? This is hard work (and a good coach can help). An entrepreneur says to you: *"I want to be gracious and compassionate in serving people—but telling people what I charge is hard."* Or a CEO wonders, *"How can I keep our very profitable 'go-for-it!' business model and at the same time develop my team to lead and listen like coaches?"* Or a leader shares her vision with you to build a team that *"has it all."* She wants:

- *genuinely curious people with*
- *world-class talent*
- *who respect and welcome each other's backgrounds, differences, and ideas and*
- *who then come together in common cause and with core values about how they will work.*

How will you help a coachee with competing commitments like these take a breath and then make room for the layers? For more on this, listen to Robert Kegan as he talks about "immunity to change."[16]

Finally, are there self-limiting parts in play? Since we've all got these, I'll say a bit more about why this one makes us tap the brakes.

Raise your hand if you've ever been misunderstood or dismissed, failed, or felt clumsy. If you've ever come close to panic just before a big performance moment. If you've ever trash-talked and shamed yourself when your performance was less than perfect. If you've ever lectured yourself about being an imposter or too needy in a time of overwhelming challenge. If you've ever felt too self-righteous to grant forgiveness to someone. If you've ever felt too ashamed to receive forgiveness. If you've ever felt like you are fabulous just as you are and don't need to change a thing and that the status quo is the best option.

If you just raised your hand or your eyebrows, you're normal.

Each of us has a true voice, a highest truest self, a you of you's, an essence, a soul. And we also all have "parts." You know, those other voices in your head that get busy when you grow or risk or attempt change. In a zillion different ways, those voices try to help by bubble-wrapping you with excessive fear or caution. Or maybe they shame or accuse you to the point of burnout or inaction. Each of your "parts" probably has deep roots, decades-old ways of insulating you from the potential pain and hardships of growing.

But here's the rest of it: your parts have information and talents. And each part even has the capacity to heal and grow along with you, and maybe to become more helpful. Or maybe to retire.

In some schools of thought, therapists and coaches have created assessments and formulas and approaches that are intended to externalize and banish those parts (aka saboteurs, critical voices, gremlins, judges, and "automatic-negative-thoughts") and, in their places, to invite and fortify inner heroes and sages.

Through my years of practicing ministry and marriage and family therapy, and now coaching, my approach is a little different. In my faith tradition, the opposite of bad behavior isn't good behavior. It's connection, forgiveness, re-engagement, and, often, healing. We may think we want to be strong and self-contained at all times, never needing forgiveness or support, but change is more likely when we let good people see and love and even enjoy our growing edges. When we're whole and our faults don't dissuade them from caring about us. What if it works that way with these parts that badger us? My approach to working with critical voices and "parts" has been deeply influenced by the work of **Dr. Richard Schwartz**.[17]

I know that our parts get busiest and loudest in times of risk and performance and disappointment—when we get so sad or scared or mad that we don't think anything will ever be different. When I hear one of those voices in myself or in one of my coachees, rather than banish the voice I try to get curious about it. Remember? **Resistance is always full of information.** No matter the agenda, our job as coaches and coaching leaders is to help people learn the sound of their truest voice. This is far more interesting than trying to channel an imagined hero or sage.

I was working recently with a coachee I'll call Lauren. Lauren has accomplished more in one lifetime than you can imagine. Now she had hit a rough patch, and this time she said to me quite emphatically, *"I just need to buck up!"* *"I just need to do something!"* *"I try to be brave."* As I listened to those emphatic statements, they just didn't sound like Lauren's true voice. They sounded like the words of a scared and tireless taskmaster. Probably since childhood that part had labored to protect her with the message that her ceaseless performing would ensure her ability to survive and get love.

But then Lauren took a breath, and, with tears in her eyes, her voice changed from harsh to soft and calm. She confessed that *"it feels like my head is underwater and as soon as I come up for air, I get dunked again."* I leaned in and asked gently, *"Are you just imagining this rough patch?"* *"No,"* she said. *"It's real."* She got quiet and then looked up at me and said, *"I haven't gotten to know fear very well in my life. But I do know how to comfort my grandchildren when they're worried."* In that moment, I think I heard Lauren's true voice. And I told her so. And then I said simply, *"I'm right here."* Here's how the remainder of our session thoughtfully unfolded. Together we decided to get curious about that tireless taskmaster, "Ms. Buck-Up" (we gave her a nickname).

I asked Lauren how she felt about Ms. Buck-Up. Lauren appreciated what Ms. Buck-Up was trying to do but was frustrated that Ms. Buck-Up seemed to only have one strategy (which was loudly overused).

I then asked Lauren to make a few further inquiries of Ms. Buck-Up (this called for slowing our pace):

- *"What does Ms. Buck-Up think would happen if she didn't badger you all the time?"*
- *"What is she trying so hard to protect?"*
- *"How old does Ms. Buck-Up think you are?"* (Turns out Ms. Buck-Up behaved the same way today as she did when Lauren was twelve years old.)
- *"What would happen if Ms. Buck-Up didn't keep doing her job in the same way now that Lauren is a very successful grown-up?"*
- Then I asked Lauren if she could offer Ms. Buck-Up some appreciation and compassion.
- We closed with a final inquiry for Ms. Buck-Up. Lauren asked, *"If I could get better at looking after my need for survival and love—what you've tried so hard to protect—what would you do instead?"*
- We both got the impression that Ms. Buck-Up, as she listened to Lauren's true voice, might be willing to learn some more respectful and up-to-date strategies.

Throughout this process, I said what I saw and heard in Lauren's true voice. And as we debriefed, we talked about how she could stay with her true voice as she navigated this rough patch, listening to her life for useful cautions. I wondered what she could share with her supportive husband about this. Before we closed, we co-created a plan for what she would do if she started to second-guess herself that evening and experience an "emotional hangover." This was hard work!

I had a friend who used to work for the US Treasury Department. As part of her training, she had to learn to identify counterfeit money. *"What did you learn to look for?"* I asked. She smiled and said, *"We mostly just got very familiar with the real thing."*

Lauren is learning the sound of the real thing, of her own true voice—her own "deep-down" that will continue to grow until the last breath she takes. This may be where spirituality comes in. Life is short and life is big, and if you are willing to face yourself and to grow, to stay safe enough, and to listen and forgive and be forgiven, your "deep-down" voice gets more resonant, more reflective of grace and truth with both yourself and others. You start to hear it more distinctly. Two ideas:

1. Listen for the tone of your true voice. If you believe in a loving God, that voice will usually be congruent with your own true voice (in my experience, good theology syncs with good psychology): it is specific, calm, constructive, respectful, gracious, truthful, timely, and life-giving. Ask yourself, ***Does this voice support and challenge me to get to where I want to go?***

2. And second, if you're scared and doubting yourself, maybe there's a reframe. Maybe your concern points to something you deeply value or need to learn. For example, that upcoming workshop you're working on. I bet at least part of your over-preparation comes from how much you want to bring great work to your team, employees, or coachees. Take a breath and let that truth become primary. Is this a caution you can use? Maybe you just need to reassure that part that's growing with you— the one that used to think you were still twelve years old—that you've got this. Then get back to work that is big enough to matter.

Yes. Resistance is always full of information.

Key Coaching Skills and Behaviors

Part 3/Finding the Next Step, the Experiment

People look to us as coaches to help them create specific, actionable movement in their lives. Vague aspirations may feel safe, but they're not very useful. As you explore what's possible and desirable in your coachee's heart and mind, get curious in your own way about things like, *"What part of this can you do now? What can you fix or keep? What needs to end or be left behind? When will you do it? Whom will you tell? Do you have enough of a plan?"* Talk about the role of accountability in coaching in your first few sessions. Like with the word **feedback**, your coachee may have an unhappy history with the word **accountability**. In coaching, accountability simply means that we're taking our coachee very seriously, caring deeply about both what they say they will do as they move forward and how they will do so.

Given a solid and growing alliance, our job is to track—graciously and steadily—with what they say they want and will do.

Your coachee will begin to pay attention to potential next steps as much as you do. As negotiated experiments emerge, I tend to get curious about them at both the close of a session and the start of the session that follows. And when the person I'm coaching "fails," I might ask, *"What did you do instead?"* or *"What are you saying to yourself about that?"*

Leveraging the coachee's values, strengths, energy. The coaching partnership assesses, explores, understands, and builds on these things in the service of the agenda and next step. Assessments fit with this skill, but they are always supplemental to the work that happens between coachee and coach. A good assessment doesn't provide answers as much as it points toward what to explore with individuals and teams. (If you use an assessment, find out if you first need to be trained in its use.)

Using the bright spots and positively defining stories of the person, group, or team you're coaching. I know, I know. Coaching is more about the present and the future than a trip in the way-back machine. But, as the old Irish saying goes, *"The thing about the past is it's not the past."* And there are times when a glance back fuels a person's gaze at his or her next steps. Each of the people we coach has stories about times when they overcame a challenge and found out what they are capable of. These are the unforgettable, even searing, experiences that underscore values, character, effort, and strength. They may also have stories that are ready for new meaning. It's not what happened to you; it's how you make sense of what happened to you. I use this skill with teams when I ask members to tell a story about one of their defining moments growing up—a story that still informs and energizes the way they show up today. Again, think "gaze-glance."

Requesting/challenging. The coach offers the coachee a specific request or challenge or powerful question based on

- The possibilities and goals that the partnership has explored in the session, or
- The coach's own wisdom and experience. This isn't the same thing as giving advice, because the coach invites evaluation and leaves the authority for the next step with the coachee. For an excellent example of a coach-flavored psychologist doing this, listen to **the TED talk by Meg Jay addressed to people in their twenties.**[18]

A good request or challenge is specific, and sometimes it's an uncomfortable stretch. But it's not an assignment—the coachee isn't obligated to grant the coach's wish. Instead, ask your coachee to consider the request/challenge and then to respond with a ***yes, a no, or a counteroffer***. Sometimes a request/challenge is simply a powerful question, asked graciously. A question that exposes more truth. *"I have a big question here. OK if I ask it?"* This is not the same thing as "assigning homework" (which I don't do).

Brainstorming/edge-storming. Use this skill when your coachee gets stuck. It's a way of exploring ***"what a coachee didn't know that they knew,"*** of new possibilities. It's a way of challenging the boundaries of your coachee's known world. Edge-storming is a little like brainstorming, but it focuses more on expanding the coachee's comfort zone, depth of experience, and expertise rather than going completely "blue sky." Think, ***A 10-percent shift.*** When I use this skill, I invite the person I'm coaching into a couple minutes of creative back-and-forth with me (***"You could . . ., I could . . ."***). Together we build a menu of possibilities.

A tangible metaphor. As your coachee identifies a strength, a gift, a relationship, an aspiration, a value, or a goal, ask, ***"Is there something you could carry, wear, experience, or see several times a day as a tactile, visual, or visceral reminder of that?"*** The answer is almost always a creative totem of their best self (collages, calendars, post-it notes, a piece of jewelry, messages on voice mail, a smooth stone in the pocket, alerts). Some tangible metaphors are defining events like weddings or graduations or funerals (*"What will you leave behind as a legacy?"* or *"What needs to just be buried with you?"*).

Some tangible metaphors are personal memorials of those moments in life after which you know things will never be the same.

Evaluating. As a coaching skill, evaluating is about establishing and maintaining your coaching alliance, agreements, and agenda—and about growing awareness. **Starting with your first interaction with a potential coachee, let them experience you as a coach.** Begin to find out about their meta-agenda. Get a glimpse of potential small steps along the way. Maybe your engagement will be long. Maybe brief. Either way, their awareness will grow, so pay attention to your coachee's emerging hopes, destinations, markers, and outcomes.

You will learn to begin with the end in mind.

These five questions that we talked about earlier in the *Playbook* are not a magic formula, and you don't have to ask them in order. In fact, your coachee may answer some of them before you ask. Your job is simply to uncover the answers in a way that fits your style and the co-creation of a coaching conversation:

1. *"What would you like to work on?"* Listen for their best hopes and aspirations.
2. *"How will you know we are making progress? If we hit the nail on the head in the next 30 minutes, what would you have? If this conversation helps, what will shift? What will be clear that seems fuzzy now? How will you know when you have it?"*
3. *"What are the strengths and values you could bring to this opportunity/challenge?"*
4. *"Who else is in your thinking as we talk about this?"* (The answers may surprise you.)
5. *"How is this big enough to matter to you in the larger scheme of things (to your vision and values)?"* **Hope is a combination of vision + self-efficacy, and it is powerful.** Remember, when you are first curious and unhurried about your coachee's best hopes and aspirations, you help them to create a "tailwind" for then resolving problems and obstacles.

And along the way you might ask, *"What are you taking away?"* or *"What do you have now that you didn't before?"* As your alliance grows and your coachee's agenda deepens, you will likely bring up how your coaching agreement is evolving too: *"When we met three months ago, you had made the decision to move to Seattle. You've made so much happen. How do you see your next steps?"*

The goal is to refresh your agenda, goals, and outcomes or to begin bringing your coaching partnership to an honorable close. **Note:** It is the mark of an unethical coach to keep himself/herself in the game without a clear mission. Both evaluating and wrapping up (see below) include having the integrity to point out when coaching isn't happening and being willing to stop.

In the SeattleCoach Stash: Listen to my four minutes on "Finding the Next Step."

Key Coaching Skills and Behaviors

Part 4/Your Authenticity, Transparency, and Presence. Being Brave.

The quality of the person you are, of your life itself, is your key instrument in this work. The Christian mystic Thomas Merton wrote, **"He who attempts to act and do things for others or for the world without deepening his own self-understanding, freedom, integrity and capacity to love, will not have anything to give others."**[19] Are you nurturing in yourself the conditions and behaviors that trust requires? Our job as coaches is to continuously grow in the way we understand our own energy, wisdom, strengths, and true moral obligations—to our own reactivity and critical voices, to our truest voice and our clearest cautions. To our own "deep-down." As coaches we pay attention to, in the words of David Brooks, both **"résumé values"** and **"eulogy values"**[20]—in our lives and in the lives of the courageous people we coach.

As a coach, will you know when you get scared or reactive or uncomfortable? Will you ask questions to which you don't already have an answer? Will you risk sounding like a fourth-grader? Will you know when you need to recover, consult, or refer? And will you find ways to be less automatic and more voluntary in what you do next? And maybe, most importantly, will you stay safe and kindhearted, calm, and resilient? Will you allow your coachee to surprise and influence you? Will you find ways to forgive? Will you build in time for some solitude and reflection—and for some patient self-coaching? This is about building your soul's agility with both grace and truth.

Bravery operates in the background of great coaches. It's the habit of routinely challenging your own comfort zone and of being willing to get out-loud about what other people in the room are probably thinking. Sometimes your job is to "take one for the team": *"Susan, every comment from you about this project has sounded tired and snarky . . ."* This isn't you diagnosing; it's more of an extension of **"saying what you see and hear."**

Ask yourself, *Do I need to be right? Or liked? Or tranquil? Or admired? Or the voice of justice? Can I stay present when things get uncomfortable?* Skilled leadership coaches learn to challenge their fears and defaults in the interest of the well-being of the people they're coaching. For example . . .

Direct communication. Sometimes we stand by our coachees by standing up to them. This, of course, means that they already know we're in their corner. My own mentor coach used to encourage me: **"Patty. Go right in there."** When you do, you may not be pleasing, but you will probably be serving. You're straightforward and uncluttered in the face of excuses and habits that inhibit the development of your coachee. Two examples: *"You got pretty loud and snarky in the meeting today. What happened just before you got loud and snarky? What did you notice about the people in the room right afterward?"* Or, *"You've mentioned to me in passing your concerns about your (weight/lack of exercise/substance abuse/unhappiness at home); what if I challenged you to take yourself more seriously about that?"*

An intuitive hit. As a coach, do you know how to listen to yourself and then speak with transparency, immediacy, and respect to your coachee? This can be a hard truth or simply a blurt, and it may take extra courage: *"Wait. What?!"* or *"I have a hunch about this. Want to hear it?"* Maybe because of your alliance you are able to bring up something that everyone else sees but may not have the courage or skill to say directly to your coachee.

Leading as the coach and "being the container." The person you are coaching chooses the agenda—that is, the destination they are hoping for. Coaches take it seriously by holding the focus and the pace, challenging distractions: *"I'd like to turn off devices for the next half-hour. OK with you?"*

Self-understanding/self-coaching. The areas in our own lives that we haven't explored or made peace with are the ones we won't tend to explore with other people. And, in addition, good coaches have some true moral judgments that make them a poor fit for some types of agenda or businesses. The challenge here is to keep growing, challenging your own comfort zone as you work with coachees when their agenda is "close to home" for you. When this happens, slow down and stay gently curious. If you feel stuck, call me or another colleague. I'll help you decide how to expand your comfort zone and, in some cases, how to refer someone to a different coach or resource.

Shut up. Shut up. Shut up. This one is a signature SeattleCoach skill probably because we're all so enthusiastic and experienced in life and we just want to help! Though it's hard for good people to stop helping, sometimes it's the respectful thing to do. Our coachees have things they're longing to say. If you can learn to let silence do some of the heavy lifting in coaching, the person you are coaching will likely grow in their awareness and they'll tell you what you want to know. Then they'll thank you. Personally, when I discipline myself to breathe and wait while my coachee is processing, I think about the vivid Spanish verb *esperar*. It carries two meanings for which we don't have an equivalent in English: ***To wait. To hope.*** And then I get a little better at challenging that little voice in my head that insists that I know and they don't. So often I'm wrong.

Speak up. Speak up. Speak up. On the other hand, maybe if you are enthusiastic but more of an introvert, the challenge might be—again in the words of one of my mentor coaches—*"Patty! Go right in there!"*

What else? Can you say more? Tell me more. Keep going. When you use one of these invitations, your coachee gets to refine the direction of the conversation—maybe even help you understand things better before you ask a question. (This skill is especially useful with coachees who tend to be people of few words but who may feel things very deeply.)

Recovering your focus. When you know that you 've lost focus as the coach or that your own triggers or gremlins have been busy and you need to recover: Notice it—not necessarily why. Just **notice** it. **Name** it out loud: *"I just lost you. I think I went away for a moment."* And **reconnect**—bring your attention back to your coachee. Your transparency might even deepen the alliance.

Coaching postures. Every coach has a **"default"** posture—the one you reach for first. Of the four postures below, which is your go-to? And what would it take to practice more fluency with the other three?

- **The Supporter**
  Leaning in: Attending, listening. Interesting factoid: studies show that women coaching together may prefer this one as a starting point.

- **The Challenger**
  Sitting forward and tall: Disagreeing graciously. What does your posture look like when you do this with someone you care about? For me, it's usually a tall, relaxed posture with soft eye contact.

- **The Witness**
  Sitting back: Waiting. Taking it in. See "witnessing" (below).

- **The Companion**

    Looking together: You know those rich conversations you've had in cars and on walks, where you and the other person look outward together, side-by-side, as you connect well? That. Interesting factoid: studies show that men coaching together may prefer this one as a starting point.

Staying aware of what you want to teach people. What will you do when a coachee says, *"Can you just tell me what you'd do?"* It's flattering to be asked to console, fix, rescue, prop up, or to tell about the time when you . . . And you're not without your own opinions. Shoot, some of your opinions are even grounded in true expertise! Why not just tell them? The quick answer is that if you can *"coach the person, not the problem"* (or in the words of one SeattleCoach, *"coach the person through the problem"*), then your coachee gets to grow—and he or she gets the credit. Remember that your coachee is creative, resourceful, and responsible for their own outcomes. So, proceed with caution when you shift from coaching to advising:

1. Is this time-sensitive, and is your clear direction needed? Learn to do 30 minutes of pure coaching before you start advising or consulting. It's a gamble, but people will surprise you with the wisdom and resources they didn't know they had—or are ready to explore.
2. In your self-coaching/self-management, pay attention to what you long to teach people so that you can be very chosen and deliberate about using that stuff. A coachee is far more inspired by the coach who asks a great, constructive question than by a coach who's thinking, *I know and you don't.*
3. And when you do offer expertise, invite your coachee's evaluation of it.

Witnessing. In her lovely novel *Gilead*, Marilynne Robinson talks about the "incandescence" of a moment "when the charm of a thing strikes you."[21] Sometimes we are the first to see or hear something very special in the life of a person we're coaching. It might be a story, a plan, a success, or a heartbreak. Or a moment when we catch them being brilliant. When those moments come, without intruding or making the moment about us, we witness. We recognize we're on sacred ground. And the person we're coaching gets to see the influence of their life on our own.

Statements of Impact. The people we coach influence us, inspire us, and teach us things. They might even irritate us with a habit or a word. A statement of impact happens when the coach speaks directly about his or her personal and immediate response to being with the coachee. As always, ask permission: *"Can I tell you how this lands on me?" "Your energy about this inspires me." "Your words are a little jolting to me." "I just got tears in my eyes too."* A statement of impact doesn't mean you continue on into a judgment, an interpretation, or a lecture. It's just you, as the coach, saying what maybe a lot of other people in your coachee's life don't or won't say.

A Statement of Impact usually means I've caught my coachee in the act of being brilliant or transparent or visionary about their life. And when I mark the moment, they will remember it: they have just "emotionally rehearsed" something important with me—something that will play soon in live action.

In the SeattleCoach Stash: Listen to my five minutes on "When Someone Asks a Coach for Advice."[m]

In the SeattleCoach Stash: Listen to four minutes about the story of "The NASA Dreamer: What Should You Do When You Get Worried about Where Your Coachee Is Headed?"[n]

Key Coaching Skills and Behaviors

Part 5/Skills to Use Strategically and Powerfully

You won't use these skills in every session, but when you do, they will be powerful. Think of them as the red pepper flakes in your co-creation.

The Miracle Question. This skill is a gift to us from the practice of Solution-Focused Brief Therapy (SFBT), a systems therapy that emerged in the 1980s. Steve de Shazer and Insoo Kim Berg were ahead of their time in inviting their therapy clients to focus not on the past but on what they wanted to achieve today.

Coaches who learn to ask the Miracle Question well are able to invite coachees to engage their imagination, ambition, hope, and courage. Ask permission and proceed gently: *"Imagine that after you leave here, move through the rest of your day, and then head to bed, while you're sleeping tonight, a miracle occurs that accelerates the best outcomes we've talked about. When you wake up tomorrow, what would you begin to notice that would tell you things are different? What would the specific evidence be as you begin to walk through your day?"* **Then slow down and explore.**

Take a few minutes to listen to a brief video about The Miracle Question by gifted therapist Elliot Connie.[22]

Championing. When your coachee is ready to take on something big but doubts himself at the last minute, try asking questions to which you know he or she must answer **yes:** *"Do you have support? Did you think this through? Have you worked your butt off? Do you know how to be a great teammate? Do you have the skills? Do you want this? Are you a good person?"* After a few nods, be quiet and see what happens. (This is not the same thing as excessive cheerleading.) *And here's a tip: when you, the coach, are the one who needs a little championing, try speaking to yourself in the second or third person: Have you worked your butt off? Has (your name) really worked his/her butt off?*

Helping your coachee to reground. As trust and movement grow, it's normal for our coachees to have sessions in which they feel especially open or emotional. This is the skill of using your own authenticity to help them regroup, to "know where the ground is" before they leave the conversation with you. They stay aware of what they've felt and accomplished in their work with you but are ready to rejoin the normal pace of life as they begin to metabolize it. Ask them what they will do to be gracious with themselves in the hours ahead. Keep an eye on the clock, and make sure you leave enough time to do this. Maybe invite a follow-up email or phone call.

"What I know about you." There are times when you look your coachee in the eye and speak directly about what you see in their character, aspirations, courage, and potential. This is another way of standing up for the person you're coaching as they consider a crucial next step. (This is not the same thing as excessive cheerleading.)

And equally powerful, *"What don't I know about you?"*

Wrapping up. (See "Evaluating" above.) When I conclude a coaching agreement, I build in time to gently acknowledge and celebrate what my coachee has accomplished. And, if possible, I assure them of my future availability to work with them on new challenges and opportunities that turn up in their life.

Coaching Skills and Presence Meet Brain Science

My Conversations with Dr. John Medina, Author of the *Brain Rules* books.

The famous anthropologist Margaret Mead was asked by a student what she considered to be the first sign of civilization in a culture. The student expected Mead to talk about fishhooks or clay pots or grinding stones. But no.

Mead said that the first sign of civilization in an ancient culture was a femur (thighbone) that had been broken and then had healed. Mead explained that in the animal kingdom, if you break your leg, you die. You cannot run from danger, get to the river for a drink or hunt for food. You are meat for prowling beasts. Without help, no animal survives a broken leg long enough for the bone to heal. That only happens when the animal does not get left behind.

As recounted in 1980 by one of Mead's students, Dr. Paul Brand.

Whether true or apocryphal, it seems believable.

Early in the development of "**Coaching for Leaders**," I started wondering what Dr. John Medina, an old friend of mine, would think of the lessons I teach about coaching skills and presence.

Through our years of friendship and shared projects, John and I—each in our own ways—have arrived at a deep understanding of how human beings like to build trust, to connect, and to co-create. I am a systems therapist and executive coach; John is a developmental molecular biologist and brain scientist. Though we come from very different areas of subject matter expertise, we have arrived at some shared truths. For example, we know (from both experience and research) that . . .

1. *When we are talking with someone, we would rather they respond to us with curiosity instead of shifting the focus to their own story or experience.*
2. *Groups and teams that foster conversational turn-taking do better.*
3. *Brains need breaks from screens (and naps are important)—and that, whether or not we develop good habits in the virtual workspace, our bodies and hearts feel the impact.*
4. *In the experience of unresolved conflict, raised voices, and/or coarse language, most people need about 30 minutes to calm down and reengage.*
5. *The place of cognitive and affective empathy is important—and that thoughtful leaders learn to develop more of it.*
6. *Leaders who get the best overall feedback scores know (1) "how to make the trains run on time" and (2) "how to be pastoral."*
7. *When women are present, groups and teams usually do better.*
8. *If you believe in God, it's better to believe in a faithful and loving God than in a punitive God who is usually unhappy with you.*

John and I both know that these practices are true. The difference is that while I mostly tell stories to make my points, John, a neuroscientist, looks at the research and studies the data. When I get excited about a new coaching "best practice" and then run it by Dr. Grumpy (John's nickname), he wants the evidence. ***"Patty, is that a hunch? An observation? Did you just make that up?"*** More than a few times he has uncovered research that underscores my observation. It is a good partnership. John has influenced me, and I want him to influence you too.

At one of our lunches, I asked Dr. Grumpy what has inspired his enduring interest in the work we both do. In the conversation that ensued, my friend of thirty-five years talked about two big reasons, which I later asked him to record for me:

> *First, you won't work in the field of cognitive neuroscience for long without realizing how ridiculously relational our brains are. That fact has fascinated me literally for decades. Adults interacting with other adults is one of the chewy centers of that interest, and coaching is an excellent way to see it in action. Whenever adults get together, they self-organize in very particular, measurable ways. This organizational tendency is so stable it can be traced to the stone age.*

> *My second reason, also relational in nature, comes from knowing you, Patty, literally for decades. People who know you experience your warmth, intelligence, your desire to make a positive difference in the lives of people. I have been able to witness this for almost 35 years.*

> *So, from a field for which I have had a life-long interest, to working with a person with whom I share a long, happy history, I am simply delighted to be in this conversation about coaching skills and behaviors—and why our brains like them so much!*

In the SeattleCoach Stash: *Listen to the point-counterpoint series of conversations in which Dr. John Medina and I discuss how brain science data support excellent coaching skills, behaviors, and presence.*°

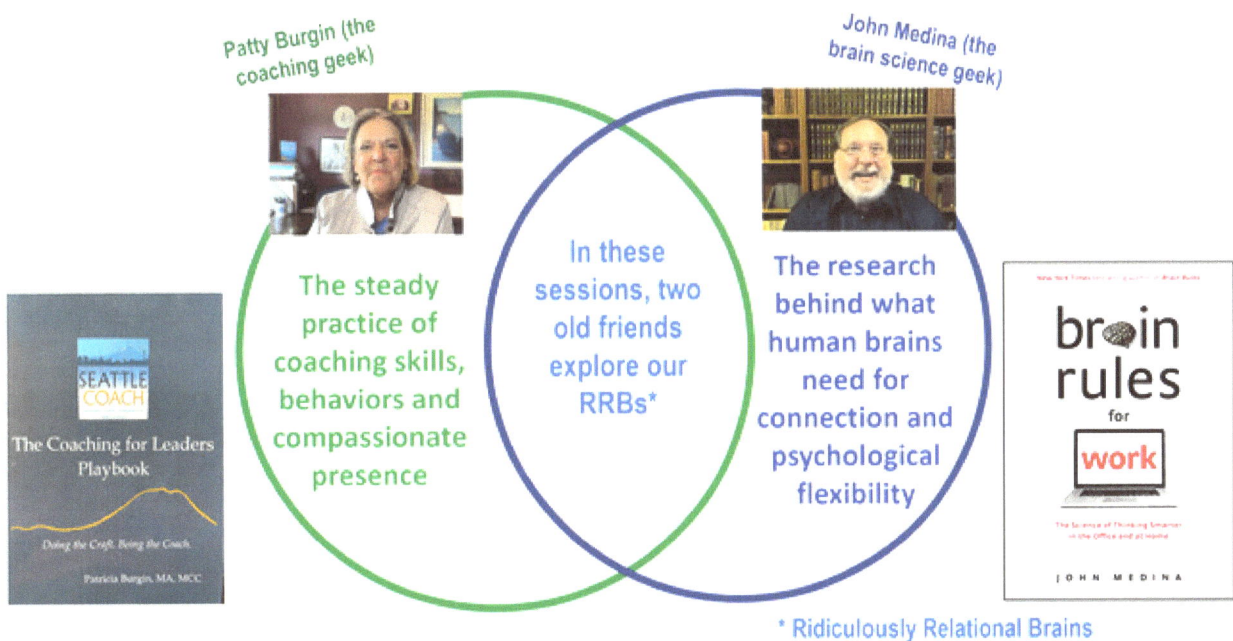

Patty Burgin (the coaching geek)

John Medina (the brain science geek)

The steady practice of coaching skills, behaviors and compassionate presence

In these sessions, two old friends explore our RRBs*

The research behind what human brains need for connection and psychological flexibility

The Coaching for Leaders Playbook

brain rules for work

* Ridiculously Relational Brains

Putting It All Together

The Arc of a Solid Coaching Conversation
(Even a brief one)

At each phase, when your agreement is to coach, "show up like a coach"—remembering that your calm and authoritative presence is your most important instrument. Throughout, you are connecting and attuning to your coachee. As trust grows, so does collaboration. You find the right pace and attend to the partnership's deepening

- Alliance ("signal strength")
- Agreement (initially, and along the way)
- Agenda (your coachee's focus, hope, destination, outcome, or personal development/desired competency—and why it matters)

The Beginning: Setting the Stage for Deepening Trust and Exploration

In the first minutes your job is to establish or deepen a partnership of trust with your potential coachee. With a strong alliance in place, you can begin to explore the agenda that is alive in their thinking—usually more about their purpose and possibilities than just about a presenting problem. Maybe the coachee has granted your wish and sent you a focus form or pre-session note. But even if they haven't, you gently explore your own version of the **Five Questions** (below) in the first several minutes. You are both attentive and unhurried. It isn't a formula. Your coachee may catch on to your interest in their answers to the **Five Questions**. Maybe they will begin to share their thoughts with you even before you ask.

Five Questions

1. *"What are you ready to work on—or even starting to be ready to work on?"* Listen for their best hopes and aspirations.
2. *"How will you know we are making progress? If we hit the nail on the head in the next 30 minutes, what would you have? What would the evidence be? If this conversation helps, what will shift? What will be clear that seems fuzzy now? How will you know when you have it?"*
3. *"What are the personal strengths and values you could bring to this opportunity/challenge?"*
4. *"Who else is in your thinking as we talk about this?"* (The answers may surprise you.)
5. *"How is this big enough to matter to you in the larger scheme of things (to your vision and values)?"*

If you and your coachee are hikers, you are helping them to choose a trailhead or destination. Maybe your focus moves to a waypoint: *"An intermediate point or place on a route or line of travel, a stopping point or point at which course is changed"* (Wikipedia).

The Middle: Exploration, "Double-Clicking," and Finding What's Possible

Always aim for mutual equality and transparency. You are fully connected to who the coachee is, how they learn and what they have to teach you. You are focused and at ease, ready to be surprised, delighted, influenced.

- The purpose of exploration is to help your coachee forward and deepen their awareness.
- Ask more questions to which you do not have the answer. Be OK with not knowing.
- Make your questions simple, direct, unembellished. Wait for them to land. If you know it's a good one, maybe ask it a second time.
- Return to check if the coaching conversation is continuing to serve the purpose and measures of success. Adjust if necessary: *"What are you taking away? What do you want right now?"*
- Say what you see. Comment directly on your coachee's limiting beliefs and behaviors. Invite your coachees to use their own intuition as a tool to come back to themselves in deeper and deeper ways. *"What do you want? What prevents you? Is there something that will shift?"*
- Let the coachee lead. Keep extending that invitation to him/her.
- Use skillful, patient questions when necessary to come back to the agenda and agreement.
- When you offer a specific acknowledgment (like when you catch them being brilliant), let it land. Let your coachee get your *"wow."*
- Let your coachee work a little harder, go a little further, or maybe down a layer.
- Ask direct, evocative, and open questions that reflect the coachee's style and thinking and strengths.
- Use generative silence to do some of the heavy lifting. Are you OK with not knowing? Help your coachee find deeper contact with the known and the unknown. Glance together at the past if that story serves the current conversation.
- Bookmark your coachee's "I coulds" along the way. They will likely lead to useful accountabilities.

The Close: Agreeing on Experiments and Next Steps

People love it when they leave a coaching conversation with a clear and achievable next step toward a goal they feel deeply about. As always, this will fit with their stage of change. I tend to expect the people I coach to lead here too via their own intuition and methods of following up on what they aspire to.

- Explore the bookmarks and "I coulds" that have come up in the conversation.
- Explore potential experiments and next steps that fit the coachee's goals, style, pace, and stage of change as well as his or her preferred methods of being accountable.

Keep in mind your own version of some core "accountability/aspirational" questions: *"What will you do? When could you do it? Who will know? Do you need a plan?"* (These kinds of questions work better than "homework.") And remember, great actions do not have to be big and public. A coachee may decide to journal or pray or reflect between now and the next meeting.

And Finally, as the Coach, You Are Also the Container

Your focus is beyond the session-to-session agenda. You are also staying mindful of your coachee's purpose in working with you. What are their core strengths and values? Their personal and professional hopes and aspirations? Their reasons for feeling restless? And how does today's conversation connect those dots? Keeping an eye on your coachee's big picture will keep you from being trapped in the tactical. (Getting trapped in the tactical is boring.) You'll end up addressing obstacles and problems but with hope and vision— and even the possibility of personal renewal—as your tailwind. Remember, you're coaching the person, not the problem.

Putting It All Together

Coaching Lab I: A Strong Start

The beginning is the most important part of the work. —Plato, The Republic

We're about to put you under the spotlight with the goal of landing a great first few minutes of coaching conversation. The purpose of this exercise is ***not*** to do a full session in four minutes. Rather, the challenge is for you to use **The Core Four** (Respect, Energy, Acknowledgment, Listening) to explore and deepen **Alliance, Agreement,** and **Agenda** and to co-create the foundation of an effective coaching conversation of any length—establishing "the purpose of these next 30 minutes," exploring what your coachee would like to have when you wrap up, and maybe why it matters.

You know that visceral sense you get when you've set the stage well? When the table is set? You've established the conditions for a safe and welcoming conversation and you've got a solid sense of the right direction, of what needs to happen next, of signal strength. You understand both what your coachee is hoping for and what success looks like, the right ingredients are at hand, and you've got the confidence to improvise if need be. That's the gut sense I want you to have when you've co-created the start of an effective coaching conversation of any length, even a brief one.

Think of these four minutes as an exercise, a rehearsal. You'll have up to four minutes to accomplish a strong start—but it may not take that long, so feel free to stop when you know you have established a solid foundation for the conversation. Maybe we'll stop you when we see that you've got it. When you're the coachee, please bring an agenda from your own growing edge.

As you begin to explore your connection, along with focus and purpose, you can trust that the conversation will unfold and deepen throughout the full session.

Before it's your turn, think about how you'd prepare for a coaching session in real life:

- You would do a little personal resetting.
- You would review any notes and next steps from prior sessions.
- You would act as "host" from the first moments of the conversation.

From the very beginning, remember that you and your coachee are collaborating on the following:

The Coaching Alliance. A full partnership, with deep and clear signal strength, in which the coachee is the ultimate decision-maker and the coach is connected, curious, and challenging. Your optimism and hope will be contagious.

Clear Agreements. About time, location, logistics.

The Coachee's Agenda. You explore what the coachee wants to work on and the markers of success. As those things are clarified, you explore further what strengths you will bring, who else is in your thinking, and how this is big enough to matter for you.

And about the Five Questions. They aren't a formula. Keep them in mind, stay curious and unhurried about each one as it makes sense in the conversation. Maybe your coachee will answer before you ask.

Here's how it will go:

- We'll ask you which specific key skills and behaviors you're working on (both categories and specifics)
- Then you will have about four minutes (we'll call time if you get to five minutes)
- If you feel stuck, do the touchdown move. We'll give you an idea.

Then we'll debrief:

First with your coachee, then with you—the coach—then with the rest of your Triad. Then your Triad Coach will comment on where you were brilliant and what you should keep doing. Maybe on something to work on going forward.

As always, breathe. Be kind to yourself as you step into and practice your coaching presence. Listen to a recording of me doing this for the "Real Coaching Sessions Unplugged" podcast hosted by Sheri Boone. Listen to the way my coachee and I begin—through about the first 7'30."[23]

BTW . . .

Again, think of Coaching Lab I as a drill, a dress rehearsal.

We know that in real life you may spend extra time at the beginning of the first few sessions getting to know your coachee, talking about expectations, and building trust.

We know that in real life sometimes even coachees with whom you have a strong alliance need extra time to "clear the deck" or to tell you an important story.

And we know that if you can consistently accomplish a strong start, even in around five minutes, you will deepen your ability to build a trusted container for a fully co-created coaching relationship.

In the SeattleCoach Stash: Listen to my three minutes about preparing for Coaching Lab I.[p]

Putting It All Together

Coaching Lab II: A Complete 10-Minute Coaching Conversation

In Coaching Lab I, we asked you to focus for up to four minutes on the beginning of a strong coaching conversation (of any length), establishing the agenda, the markers of success, and maybe exploring why it matters to your coachee.

Sometimes our coachees need to touch base between conversations. And whether you are an internal coach and someone has caught you for a few minutes between meetings, or you are coaching someone externally and they've asked for a strategic 10 minutes, a great 10 minutes can make a lot of difference. **Here is the challenge: can you still make a brief conversation a full coaching conversation?**

This is what we'll practice in Coaching Lab II. Not easy, I know, but think of this as a big learning experience—you're safe and you can't fail. And you'll get useful feedback from good people who are firmly in your corner. Do you remember reading about "feedback-ish" as we started this journey together? We'll build on that. And as you take your turn to observe and offer some coachy feedback, the "Tracking Your Key Skills and Behaviors" worksheet in the following section may be useful.

As always, the purpose of this exercise is to cultivate your ability to help the person you are coaching join you in finding the areas where exploration and experimentation are most possible and desirable, and to land a next step. This means that you

- Begin with uncovering the answers to the Five Questions (remember, you don't have to ask them as a formula);
- Ask questions that reflect your understanding of where your coachee is in the stages of change;
- Listen and explore—especially for the information in your coachee's resistance and aspirations;
- And manage the space and the pace of the session, collaborating with your coachee on the location and nature of their possible next steps.

You'll coach a peer-coaching partner you have worked with in the week(s) prior to your turn. This will probably be a different person than the person with whom you worked in Coaching Lab I. You may want to ask for a Focus Form.

Members of your Triad will use "Tracking Your Key Skills and Behaviors" (below) as they listen. If you would like to record your session and debriefing (for your own learning), bring your favorite device. When you record someone, be sure to get their permission. As always, it is fine to have notes with you.

When it's your turn:

☐ As you take the spotlight, your Triad Coach will ask a question or two: *"As you've explored the Key Skills (both the main categories and the specifics), what feels easy? What feels challenging? What's an experiment you'd like to try?"* You can also request personal feedback on something else you're working on.

☐ Then we'll ask members of your Triad, *"Who else shares those areas of ease and challenge?"*
☐ Your Triad Coach will track with you as you take the spotlight. They will ask you if you'd like to get a signal when you're in your final two minutes.

About five minutes in:

Your Triad Coach will ask you to briefly pause your conversation. He or she will be curious about one of these questions:

☐ *"How do you see the agenda so far?"*
☐ *"How do you see your next move?"*
☐ *"If you were to ask a question to help your coachee go down a layer, what could it be?"*

Then you and your coachee will continue.

At the close of your 10 minutes, we'll debrief and offer a little "feedback-ish." We will tend to keep our focus mostly on the coach, less on the coachee's story:

☐ Again, we'll start with the coachee *("What worked? Is there anything your coach could have done more of?")*
☐ Then move to you, the coach *("Tell us about your thinking . . .")*
☐ Then we'll turn to the members of your Cohort with whom you have some shared areas of focus.
☐ Then your Triad Coach will give you their feedback. And since showing is better than telling, if your Triad Coach has given you challenging feedback, you have the option of asking them to *"step into my shoes and enact what you might try instead in the situation."*
☐ Finally (because we're coaches), we might ask what you're taking away.

You may find it useful to go back to the recording from the "Real Coaching Sessions Unplugged" podcast and listen to the way my coachee and I navigate a brief session through about the first 28 minutes. Optionally, an interview with the host follows our "session" from 27:41 to 52:15.[24]

> **Breathe. And be kind to yourself as you practice both your coaching skills and presence.**

In the SeattleCoach Stash: *Listen to my three minutes about preparing for Coaching Lab II.*[q]

Putting It All Together

Tracking Your Key Skills and Behaviors

The Coachee's Stage of Change

☐ *What's your theory? Did the coach's questions fit? Support? Challenge?*

The A's

☐ **The Coaching Alliance:** *Is there a full partnership in which the coachee is safe enough to fully engage with the coach? Is the coachee the ultimate decision-maker? Is the coach is connected and open?*
☐ **A Clear Agreement:** *Is there clarity about the what, the how, the scope?*
☐ **The Coachee's Agenda:** *As an observer could you tell what it was?*

The Arc—and Finding a Next Step: What did you notice?

How did the coach collaborate with the coachee to explore the agenda—and to stay curious and timely about a possible and desirable next step?

The "Core Four"

☐ **Respect**   *Coaches express and embody respect for their coachee's goals, agenda, permissions, confidences and resourcefulness.*

☐ **Energy**   *Coaches study and use their personal energy, judgment, experience, and intuition. They are aware of their own triggers and agenda and they use their own voice, mood, breath, and posture in being present.*

☐ **Acknowledgment**
          Coaches acknowledge the admirable, saying what they see in the character, actions, strengths, self-responsibility, and vision of others. Their words are genuine and clear, marked by both grace (support) and truth (directness and challenge).

☐ **Listening**   *When a strong coach listens well—usually beyond the actual words—they inspire clarity, energy, and possibility. They evoke awareness.*

Key Skills	Used	Might Have Used
Co-creating a Level 3 Conversation		
Saying what you see and hear	_____	_____
"Reset" / Finding the focus	_____	_____
Clearing the deck	_____	_____
Finding the right pace	_____	_____
Clarifying focus	_____	_____
Meta-view	_____	_____
Metaphor	_____	_____
Time-out	_____	_____
Bottom line	_____	_____
Reframing	_____	_____
Level 3 questioning	_____	_____
An inquiry	_____	_____
Exploring Resistance		
Old and potentially limiting stories?	_____	_____
Missing resources?	_____	_____
Stage of change?	_____	_____
Competing commitments?	_____	_____
Critical voices?	_____	_____
Find the Next Step, the Experiment		
Leveraging the coachee's values, strengths, energy	_____	_____
Using the coachee's bright spots and positively defining stories	_____	_____
Requesting/challenging	_____	_____
Brainstorming/edge-storming (the 10-percent shift)	_____	_____
A tangible metaphor	_____	_____
Evaluating *("What are you taking away?")*	_____	_____

Your Authenticity, Transparency, and Presence. Being Brave.

Direct communication   _____   _____

An intuitive hit   _____   _____

Leading as the coach and "being the container"   _____   _____

Self-understanding/self-coaching   _____   _____

Shut up. Shut up. Shut up.   _____   _____

Speak up. Speak up. Speak up.   _____   _____

What else? Can you say more? Tell me more. Keep going.   _____   _____

Recovering your focus   _____   _____

Coaching postures   _____   _____

Staying aware of what you want to teach people   _____   _____

Witnessing   _____   _____

Statements of Impact   _____   _____

The Miracle Question   _____   _____

Championing   _____   _____

Helping your coachee to reground   _____   _____

"What I know about you"   _____   _____

"What don't I know about you?"   _____   _____

Wrapping up   _____   _____

Your observations?

A Word about Coaching Ethics

When you break the big laws, you do not get liberty; you do not even get anarchy. You get the small laws.
—G. K. Chesterton, English writer, poet, philosopher, dramatist, journalist, and theologian

Laws. Rules. Principles. Morals. Ethics. Those aren't really synonyms, are they?

As in all of life, it matters in leadership coaching that people have a high opinion of your essential integrity, kindness, trustworthiness, and good faith. Staying on course ethically is mostly about your common sense, your courtesy, your character, and "not breaking the big laws."

Make a practice of being better than you need to be and of staying current in your growth and professionalism.

1. **Confidentiality.** That is, taking good care of other people's information.
2. **Documentation.** Think "minimal and essential" if you keep notes. I tend to track agenda, outcomes, and great quotable quotes.
3. **Agreements.** Whether or not your agreements are in writing, good ones invite collaboration, predictability, and trust.
4. **Having Allies.** In addition to sharpening your craft, allies help you stay aware of your values, strengths, and growing edges. They will help you know when it's time to ask for help.*
5. **Awareness of risk**. How close is what you are doing to psychotherapy? How vulnerable is your coachee? As with all risk assessment, follow your intuition and good judgment, asking, "What could go wrong?"

The Biggest Rookie Mistakes/Complaints

- Having unclear agreements.
- Lack of confidentiality; not taking respectful care of your notes.
- Being socially or sexually inappropriate with someone you're coaching. (But you knew that.)
- Forgetting to be genuine, kind, and courteous.
- Even if you do not think of yourself as having bias, there are probably things that come up that make you stop listening and start reacting and defending and moving to your own agenda. That's normal, but part of your job is to be aware of when it happens and what you will do about it. Level 3 listening is the opposite of "reloading." It doesn't mean that you don't hold your own values and convictions closely; it just means that, as a coach or coaching leader, you stay curious—maybe extra specifically curious—about what you're seeing and hearing.
- Not listening to your gut and awareness of risk *("What could possibly go wrong?").*
- Not growing, consulting, and building a trusted network of colleagues.
- Not referring a coachee when they would be better served by another professional.

*When to Bring in Your Allies

- Regularly.
- When you're stuck. Or you wonder if you might be facing a mental health issue.
- When your coachee could benefit from having another resource "on the team": a subject matter expert, a therapist, or legal counsel—or even a different coach.
- When your personal or professional boundaries begin to feel fuzzy.
- When you feel especially enthusiastic about the pleasure and results of your coaching.

Being the Coach

Your Coaching Presence
The Core of Coaching Leadership

Your Coaching Presence

Vocation is the place where the work you most need to do connects with what the world most needs to have done. —Frederick Buechner

My new coachee looks intently at me and asks, *"Now how does this work?"* We've interviewed each other, decided we are a good match, discussed his agenda and outcomes, and agreed to dig in together. I smile back, consulting for a moment that place in my heart where I keep my convictions about why this work matters so much—to me, to the organizations I support, to our culture, and to the earnest and good man looking at me.

* * * * * * * * * * *

Beyond a coaching leader's skills and behaviors and powerful questions there is coaching presence. And it, of course, begins with the way we coach ourselves.

There are few things as timeless and honored in all successful human cultures as a combination of gratitude, perspective, compassion, and responsibility-for-most-of-what-happens-to-you—all in the context of some solid human connections. As mostly mature grown-ups, we know that these things are the indispensable ingredients of our best decisions—for our mental and emotional **resilience** and agility and for developing empathy through the course of a happy life. And they are also key to every successful coaching partnership I have ever had.

Resilience vs. the Ruts

We can spot the elements of resilience (gratitude, perspective, compassion, and responsibility-for-most-of-what-happens-to-you in the context of some solid human connections) in each other from a mile away. We can also spot their absence in people who tend to be stuck in **the rut of chronic fragility**, grievance, victim identity, and entitlement. Here are three hallmarks of this rut (aka personal and team gridlock):

1. *An unceasing focus on outside causes as the reasons for their unhappiness.*
2. *Determined efforts to convert other people to their position.*
3. *And the inability (or unwillingness) to relate to people who see things differently.*

Unexamined empathy supports and aligns with people who share your biases, but it might be contemptuous of those who do not. Unexamined empathy usually fails to distinguish between offense and actual harm. Unexamined outrage is easy, reductive, and common.

Making matters worse, there is **another related rut—that tendency in our culture to get numb to the hard stuff**, getting addicted to substances and technology and to finding our main sources of comfort/dopamine outside of our relationship with ourselves, other humans, and maybe even with God. This rut reduces our immunity to what C. S. Lewis called "the problem of pain[25] and Dr. Freud called "common unhappiness."[26]

It gets worse.

If you are stuck in either rut (they tend to go together), you are less likely to have good people in your corner when you need them. You might bond with other aggrieved people who are as unhappy and mad and stuck as you are, but that gets old.

We all know older people who shine in their resilience—not because their lives have been easy. They have usually endured plenty of ordinary misery. But because of the thousands of choices they've made over time, they have developed and deepened *gratitude, perspective, compassion, and responsibility-for-most-of-what-happens-to-you* in their personalities. We all know the other kind of older person too. I think I figured this out as a child just by experiencing my two (very different) grandmothers.

This Is a Good Place to Say That Excellent Coaching Is Not . . .

1. An endlessly rosy belief in the radiant potential of human goodness.
2. A spiritual belief to "let go and let God."
3. A mantra of exclusively happy thoughts and messages.
4. The elimination of any recognition of threat, challenge, weakness, or evil (cover ears, go la-la-la).
5. Indulgence of and organization around the chronically aggrieved.

Excellent coaching has become a "thing" at this point in our Western history, I think, because there is a longing in our culture to course-correct: to regain control over our attention, to better acknowledge character and behavior, to patiently build depth, to stay present and curious in times of disagreement, and to stand up to obstacles—and even failure—coming back stronger. What if you got to bond with people that sought stuff like that?

Are You a Good Grown-up?

One of the keys to developing resilience seems to be the presence of a "good grown-up." Beyond anything else, that is what a good coach needs to be (no matter how old the coachee): a person who, as a life practice, is the architect of his or her own character, resilience, and enduring happiness; a person who listens with both grace and truth to their own life. Without that practice, there can be no reliable coaching presence with anyone else. Nor, in fact, can there be any truly ethical coaching.

Great coaches know how to earn trust. And they are contagious in their enthusiasm, not necessarily because of their command of data or technique but because of their ability to be both separate and connected. Think of a warm handshake between two mature people—clearly separate and clearly connected all at the same time. Think about how refreshing this is in a culture where involuntary handshakes—or stand-offs—are all too common. Great coaches know how to build warm-handshake relationships. Separate. Connected.

Once you begin to become a reliable coaching presence, the question becomes, *"How do you help individuals and teams develop their own warm handshakes—the ability to stay curious and connected in disagreement and crisis without insisting on the fake peace of involuntary compliance? And can you help people learn that, even as you focus with them on their outcomes?"*

We know that coachable people are quite capable of looking "below the water line" to identify and develop their strengths and sense of purpose and to explore and experiment with their obstacles, outcomes, and next steps. I know—it's true that some people are born with sturdier constitutions, or they have had the advantages of better parenting or better cultures. Some are born into families where they are either mostly ignored or mostly indulged. Both kinds of dysfunction leave children unfairly vulnerable to the ruts I mentioned and less able to recover from and course-correct from ordinary misery.

But here's the deal: no matter what the starting point, if you can help the person you are coaching to focus on their strengths, assets, and aspirations just a bit more than on their obstacles and inabilities, they can usually pursue mastery in something (along with more resilience, gratitude, perspective, compassion, and self-responsibility). It is about the ratio (keep reading). The oldest and most appreciated of storylines through the centuries goes like this: *"A hero goes on a quest."* The stories we love are stories of resilience, of overcoming obstacles, and of continuing on, stronger and wiser. They begin with a hurricane and end with hope. Do you know any great personalities who have not spent time in, and found their way through, a personal wilderness? I do not. And if you are reading this, I know you are one of them.

* * * * * * * * * * *

I looked back at the exceptional person before me. "Well," I said, "I'm the expert on some things—like asking questions that are big enough to matter and listening carefully to the answers that come back. Like uncovering and capitalizing on your strengths and stories and style. Like finding out about your vision and how you like to lead and how you see your next steps—the ones that you believe to be both possible and desirable. Like challenging you to go after the hard stuff so you can get what you want—and then watching how hard you will work. But I will always consider you to be the expert on you. This work will take great resilience." He smiled back at me, "That's exactly what I want to get better at."

Your Coaching Presence

The Coaching Leader's Arena

The story of Mentor comes from Homer's *Odyssey*. Odysseus, King of Ithaca, is preparing to march off to fight in the Trojan War—and ultimately to a wandering 10-year . . . well, odyssey. Before he leaves, he asks a wise older man to oversee his household and be a trusted advisor and protector to his young son, Telemachus, with a commission to *"teach him everything you know."* The wise older man's name? Mentor.

In the roughly three thousand years since, *Mentor* has joined our vocabulary, coming to mean something like *a trusted advisor, friend, teacher, and wise person who invests time, energy, and affection in the growth of another*. And through the millennia, gurus, maestros, wizards, pastors, priests, guides, sages, counselors, philosophers, shepherds, wise advisors, heroes, reverend mothers, saints, exemplars, pilgrims, and Jedi Masters have joined the tradition. Like any profession, there have been both geniuses and charlatans, but the best of us have found ways to care, cure, support, challenge, and talk about what it all means. Through the millennia, the human appetite for secure engagement with what we are now calling "coaches" has stayed the same. And now, in your own journey, you have become part of the story. Your hope is to use your wisdom and experience to inspire the development and purpose of others.

Here's what I love about leaders who want to learn to coach:

1. You're already great at something else: you have spent years learning subject matter expertise—your SME. SeattleCoaches are executives, lawyers, surgeons, fitness experts, parents, pastors and faith leaders, consultants, HR business partners, marketing experts, CPAs, recruiters, therapists, realtors, teachers, business owners, and adventure tour leaders.
2. And, though you may already see yourself as a mentor and coach, you came to "Coaching for Leaders" to be a learner again.
3. And you know how to honor your own point of view on things while staying curious, rather than punitive, about those of others.

The Coaching Leader's Arena: Four Quadrants

You know how a great driver in a great car shifts smoothly through the gears, hitting the right one for the right conditions at the right moment? That is how a great coach or coaching leader moves around what I call the Coaching Leader's Arena in brief conversations—in meetings with individuals, groups, and teams; and in full coaching sessions that focus on the agenda or performance of their coachee or employee.

Based on my years of coaching and training smart people, here is how I have organized my thinking about the gears, the Coaching Leader's Arena—in other words, the world into which coaches and coaching leaders step every day.

Most managers and leaders have a quadrant that is their "default" gear; for many, it's traditionally been that southwest quadrant. Then, as they begin to experiment with their personal "Coaching Gear," they become better, more versatile drivers overall.

Take a moment to let your mind wander around the quadrants below. Can you identify your current default?

You engage with Level 3
curiosity, questioning, and
listening

You, the leader, get to be the main creator or doer	Teaching, Speaking, and Inspiring	Connected and Co-Creating: Coaching
Your brain lights up	Telling, Advising, and Giving Direction	Mentoring, Sponsoring, and Introducing

Your coachee gets to be the main creator or doer

(You, the leader, challenge, support, and stay curious)

Your coachee's brain lights up

You engage mostly with
your subject matter
expertise and experience

While they continue to grow in their expertise and experience, giving direction and coping with complexity, they also learn to ask questions that are big enough to matter. And then they learn to listen for the meaning and possibility that comes back to them from the members of their teams. They usually hear deepening levels of intelligence and possibility and enthusiasm. Maybe their impulse to micromanage diminishes. One coaching leader observed, "People seem more confident when I coach them than they do when I mentor them."

The Surrounding Blue Circle: That's Your Presence

Coaching leadership presence is the foundational element to whatever "gear" you select. It includes your ability to be calm, confident, resilient, and authentic—even in the times when you are giving direction. It boosts your ability to move thoughtfully and fluently around the Arena.

> **Even as they move from gear to gear, coaching leaders find ways to be focused, connected, curious and even unhurried.**

You engage with your
"level 3" curiosity,
questioning and listening

You, the coaching leader, get to be the main creator or doer	Teaching, Speaking, and Inspiring	The Coaching Gear
Your brain lights up	Telling, Advising, and Giving Direction	Mentoring, Sponsoring, and Introducing

Your coachee/
employee gets
to be the main
creator or doer

You challenge
and support

Their brain
lights up

You engage with your
subject matter expertise
and experience

The more you become clear about what could be most useful in each moment for the individuals and teams you coach and lead, the more you open the possibility of leading from the powerful gear of that northeast corner, which, as your team matures, may become a new home base.

No matter your starting point, it takes a personal "pause button" in order to be deliberate about when and how to move into each gear. Every leader I work with has their own defaults to recognize, to use and grow from.

- Do you have a bias for action?
- Is your bias for reflection and contemplation?
- Is your bias more to challenge, or do you just love to support?
- What's important to you? (Performance? Deliverables? Business results? Employee development, satisfaction, and retention?)
- And in CFL, how will you experiment with, and even talk to your team about, your forays into the northeast quadrant?

Here is what I've noticed about executives who get good at coaching: they learn to move through the gears as needed, without ever abandoning their coaching presence. This means they understand how to bring their calm, clear coaching presence to recognizing · · ·

- Moments when they need to advise and give direction.
- Or it is time to thoughtfully mentor (when you're convinced that *I know, and they don't*)?
- Or to teach and inspire?
- Or to simply get curious and explore, *What does this coachee/employee know? What are they capable of?* Maybe they didn't know they knew—or haven't been confident enough to say.

The Surrounding Orange Circle: It's Also about the Organization

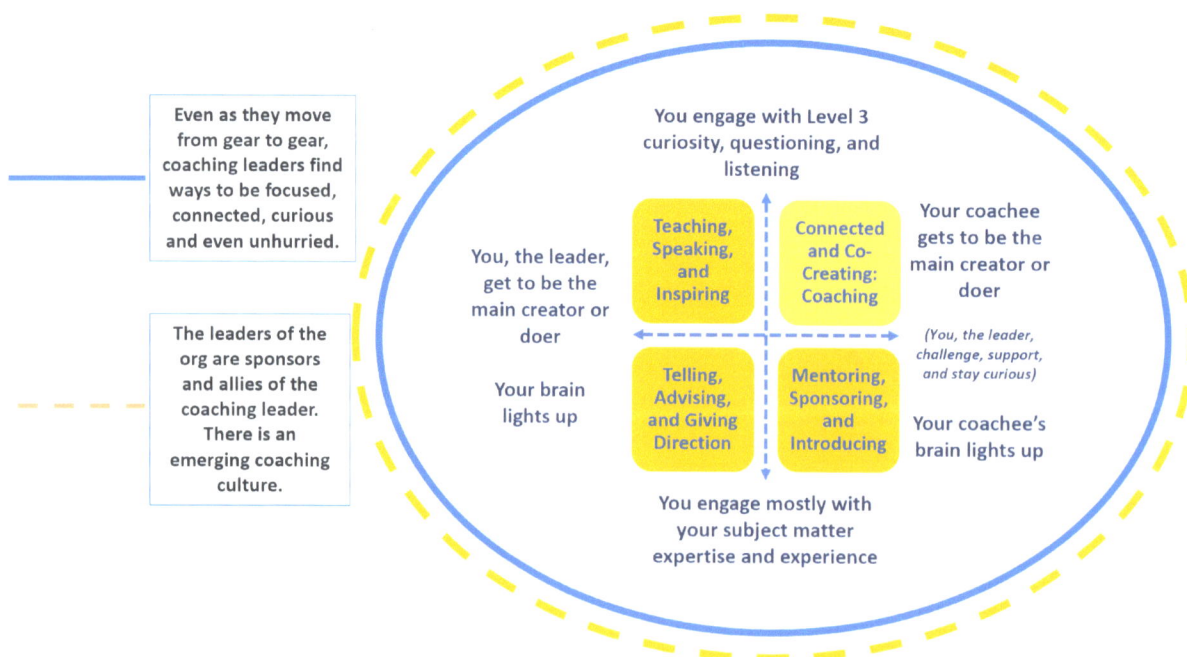

Organizations have their own defaults. Think of the surrounding orange circle as the system or culture within which the coaching is happening.

In the words of Satya Nadella, Microsoft's transformative CEO, there are "know-it-all cultures" and there are "learn-it-all cultures."[27] And both bring a compelling context. The companies I choose to work with foster both coaching presence and time to learn the skills required of leaders who invite conversations in the northeast quadrant—even brief ones.

A few years ago, I was contacted by a big company in Silicon Valley. They had heard about the work I was doing in the Northwest. "We've got twelve young new executives whom we're investing heavily in," they explained. "Could you fly down and spend the day with them? Tell them a little about coaching?"

"Sure!" I enthused. "I'll need a big, open room with windows, an executive sponsor who can join us for the day—and I'll send down a few ideas for them to start thinking about. The sponsor is important—I'll be inviting a lot of interaction, and your young leaders need to know what the bosses are thinking about coaching leadership."

Maybe I should have been nervous when three weeks later I had not heard anything further—except for an email confirming the time and place. Then, the day before our meeting, my executive sponsor emailed to say that another commitment had come up for her. "You know, Patty, we bring in a new expert for these guys every month, and they are always eager to listen. I really can't be there, but my assistant will help you find the room."

Then I did get nervous. I found my way from the San Jose airport to the right building, and the assistant met me and led me to a small, low-ceilinged, oblong, windowless room that was oriented to a big screen at one end. It was dark.

"Hey," I said. "I'd asked for a room with more light and some open space!"

"Sorry," said the assistant. "This was all that was available." And then she left.

Luckily, I did have a few slides, so I set them up. And then in walked my audience of earnest young executives with their devices out, ready for some serious notetaking.

Over the next three hours I did my best to introduce and illustrate some key concepts, but nothing I did seemed to bring interaction, evaluation, challenge, or even much curiosity. Even though I had asked them to put away their devices, they stayed intent on taking notes.

We wrapped up, everyone thanked me, and they filed out. I called for my ride back to the airport. Then I sat on the curb in front of the building waiting and blaming myself. That insulting little heckler that lives in most of our heads got busy. I had brought my calm, authoritative presence and some good content. What had gone wrong?

In retrospect, I think I had encountered a culture that was mostly operating, at least at that time, in the southwest quadrant. It was a "know-it-all" culture and was developing its emerging leaders accordingly. Maybe I had influenced them a little, but the missing experience with an executive sponsor who had some fluency with the Coaching Leader's Arena likely influenced them a lot.

In the years since, when SeattleCoach builds a partnership with a company, it is not simply to do trainings. Rather, it is to come alongside visionary leaders who are building cultures that understand the ROI of fluency around the Coaching Leader's Arena.

A Few Common Scenarios

Assume you are calmly operating from your leadership presence and that if an organizational culture is part of the picture it is supportive. Which gear (or combination of gears) would you use in the following scenarios?

1. *There is a deadline looming, and your most resourceful team members ask for some clear direction from you. It is part of your job.*
2. *You have just promoted a talented young leader, and part of her job will be to do more presenting and facilitating with customers. She worries, "I haven't done much of that. But I want to—I really want to get better."*
3. *A colleague asks, "Would you be available to come teach a workshop about [your SME]?" And you develop some great content. You also build in time and permission for your participants to interact on and evaluate what you present as they figure out how to apply their learning.*
4. *Someone asks if you have ever navigated something like the tough thing they are facing, and, though you do not talk about yourself much, you decide it might be in their interest to share part of your own story with them.*
5. *Your employee asks for your advice, but you have a hunch that he knows more than he thinks he does about what to do next.*
6. *Your colleague arrives from an emotionally intense day and cannot remember what he wanted to talk about with you.*
7. *At the end of an informational/exploratory conversation, your new coachee is curious about the structure and process of her new relationship with you and asks, **"Now, how will this work?"** And you give clear direction and recommendations for what will happen next, probably referencing how you like to work. I say things like, "I'll send you an agreement later today, along with a payment link. And before you leave, let's schedule our first couple of sessions. I've noticed through the years that people are happiest with their outcomes when we work together for about 10 hours over the course of a quarter."*
8. *Your coachee's confidence is wavering. She wonders how she can be coachable today in the face of an enormous challenge.*
9. *You are a manager who wants to lead more with coaching. Your default has been the southwest quadrant. Is it possible for you to have one-on-ones during which you occupy the northeast quadrant? How would you help your employees and your organizational system understand what you are doing?*

A great coach always has some SME, and coaching doesn't mean you have to hide the ball. The challenge is to move around the quadrants fluently and as needed while embracing and embodying your calm, connecting, curious, and clear coaching presence.

Three Questions to Think about as You Consider the Arena

1. Which quadrant (or gear) was your default before joining a "Coaching for Leaders" Cohort?
2. What could make it possible for you to operate 10 percent more from the northeast quadrant?
3. How could you be effective in each quadrant—without ever abandoning your coaching presence?

___

In the SeattleCoach Stash: Listen to my eight minutes about "From Coaching Presence to Coaching Conversations."

Your Coaching Presence

The Somatics

Somatic (from Ancient Greek, σωματικός) meaning "of the body." Think of somatics as relating to the body in all its wholeness and to its experience, conditioning, and history.

Literally, the body reflects the shape of our lives. And we have choices.

Leadership presence is not only a professional coaching competency but also something that we actively model, inspire, and foster in the lives of the people we coach. One of our bedrock beliefs as coaches is that with more trust comes more awareness and with more awareness comes more choice. And with more choice come new possibilities for where and how we'll go next in our lives. I think of awareness as having several interlocking "starting points." The last three are somatic:

1. In your beliefs and interpretations
2. In your words
3. In your breath and voice
4. In your tone, mood, and emotions
5. In your non-verbals: your posture/shape, facial expressions, and gestures

With increasing awareness from any of those starting points, we can find better direction for what we do next.

A somatic bottom line is that human brains learn best when they are safe enough. Not bubble-wrapped but safe enough to reduce vigilance and to engage, trust, challenge, and explore. As coaches, we learn to work with all kinds of temperaments while building our own emotional authenticity, agility, and resilience. The more you learn the elements of your somatic presence, the better you'll be at Level 3 conversations:

- Being a conversation partner who is safe enough to explore with (and as coaches, we know that simply offering people more data doesn't light up their brains nearly as well);
- Maintaining the good signal strength of a deep connection;
- Paying attention to all the ways the people we're working with communicate their most fundamental concerns, commitments, inspirations, fears, values, and strengths.

As we've discussed, human beings have hugely unconscious minds that process enormous amounts of information "in the background." We have evolved to pay attention to our surroundings (*"Can I eat that?" "Can it eat me?"*), and this has helped us survive and thrive.

Think about how you enter a room. What message are you "leaking?" The other people in the room are scanning and making meaning of what just came through the door: *Is there low-level danger? Do I need to brace for something? Ah, I can relax and get curious!* Or, *Things are about to get exciting!*

In other words, you're contagious. Whether you're the boss, the coach, or the person delivering coffee, you have the capacity to both set the tone in the room and correct it. This is so big that I believe the person in the room who is most aligned, congruent, and transparent somatically—and thus, trustworthy—is automatically the most influential (regardless of title). They change the energy in the room just by showing up.

The good news is that not only are you contagious but you also have power to cultivate what's catching. Think about how much time you spend preparing presentations and decks—even choosing the right words. What if you had a way of preparing your somatic presence as well, of increasing the odds that you could show up as your best self?

As a coach, you scan with some key questions in mind: *Is this person aligned? Is their message congruent? Is there integrity? Is he/she safe and confident enough to be coachable?*

As you review more details about each of the following "starting points," see if you can identify an experiment . . .

1. In Your Breath and Voice

As coaches we listen more than we talk, which gives us time to pay attention to the depth and efficiency of our breathing. The diaphragm is our main muscle of communication. When it's not working well, we choke and get scared—and that's contagious too.

Your voice is the vehicle for your thoughts—and it reveals your inner state and beliefs. And you can shape it. Our unconscious minds listen for pitch and quality, pace, and undertones. And the unconscious mind of a group makes decisions about who its influencers are.

If you're like me you can identify hundreds of voices, but a few have had a great impact on you. I began to pay attention to voice as a teenager listening to Rev. Martin Luther King and later to Ronald Reagan and Margaret Thatcher. In pivotal times in history, their voices were calm and strong, comforting, and authoritative all at the same time. The good news of this first starting point is that anyone can increase the power of his or her voice and thus become a stronger leader and coaching presence.

Try this with your breath:

Start by just noticing your breath. How far into your core does it go? Once you've noticed it, see if you can gently allow it to take up more space so that your ribcage or abdomen begin to move. You will likely find yourself sitting taller and maybe needing to stretch something.

Or try this with your voice:

Find the pitch, tone, and cadence at which your own voice feels strongest and most resonant. What can you do to bring your voice into that range? This might mean that you'll try speaking lower and slower. And what happens with your breath when you do that?

2. In Your Tone and Mood

Human emotion unconsciously helps us make sense of what's happening. If I am nervous or self-conscious, what shows up to my coachee or audience is, *"There's danger in the room."* This launches a vicious cycle between everyone's unconscious minds, which accelerates the message of danger and concern in the room. Your self-consciousness becomes their danger. The cool thing is that you can develop emotional focus for key moments. When you think about it, charisma isn't magic fairy dust sprinkled on a lucky few; it's simply emotional focus and behavioral congruence. And it just takes practice. As coaches, we know we must train ourselves to be present and to express the behaviors and emotions that fit the moment. That presence is contagious.

If you believe you have some things that are uniquely yours to say and do in your brief time on the planet, your posture, voice, face, and gestures begin to reflect it congruently. The reflexive state of an unfocused human brain is usually fear-based and scanning for trouble: *Will they like me? Will I make this time valuable? Will I lose my way?* Instead, we can literally give our brains other things to search for: *What's the opportunity? What are they hungry for? What gifts do I have for them? What else?*

Try this with one of your stories:

> Remember a time when you have been at your best with other people. You were confident, open, clear, and gracious and very effective. Think about that experience long enough to remember what it was like for you mentally, emotionally, physically, viscerally, socially. You knew you were contagious in the best of ways, and people were grateful.

> Obviously, if you can break down some of the specific elements *(I knew I was adding value, I'd prepared enough, I'd eaten well, things were great with my spouse, I liked what I was wearing, it was mid-morning, I was standing, I'd worked out that morning . . .)*, you can think about building those elements into your development plan.

> Once you've done that, notice how that memory shows up in your physical presence. Our beliefs influence how we walk into the world (and vice versa). And we can choose them.

3. In Your Non-Verbals: Your Posture/Shape, Facial Expressions, and Gestures

The quality of your voice and breath and of your mood and emotion is obviously related to your posture, movement, face, and gestures.

These things are so powerful that many transcend culture. Some even work for all primates. And we all know that posture, movements, face, and gestures beat content when we are not aligned.

Try this with your posture:

> Whether you're seated or standing, gently move your posture into the one your grandmother probably taught you: at your full stature, shoulders relaxed and giving your lungs room, head balanced, face relaxed, arms uncrossed. This posture signals openness and trust—and trustworthiness.

Remember

You've spent hours in coach training developing your skills and how you will talk about your work. What would happen if you found deeper ways for your mind and mood, your body and behavior to be even more aligned? Since everything is interactive, start with the part of Somatic Presence that feels most interesting for you to experiment with and remember:

- Your presence will always beat your content when the two are not aligned,
- Greater awareness brings more choice, and
- As a coach and leader, you are contagious—and you have power to cultivate what's catching.

My bottom line on somatic awareness: Pick a starting point that's interesting to you. Then test and learn, notice what is good and useful, connecting, and life-giving. Repeat. As you think about these things, the resource below might be useful to you.

In the SeattleCoach Stash PDF***:*** *Listen to Amy Cuddy's viral TED Talk, "Your Body Language May Shape Who You Are."*[28]

Your Coaching Presence

Coaching Big Emotions (and with them)

When you listen with empathy to another person, you give that person psychological air. —Stephen R. Covey

When feelings are mentionable and manageable, it is a great service to mental health. —Fred Rogers

As I went through coach training myself years ago, I continued to practice as a marriage and family therapist. And as I began to coach a few hours a week, I wondered, *Would these conversations be just as poignant, emotional, and purpose-driven? Would they be as significant, even healing? And would I grow in my ability to stay emotionally and somatically present with the people I wanted to serve?*

As a coach, would I continue to understand my strengths and values? My triggers? What my yes's and no's should be? My sense of what makes me a blessing and what makes me annoying? Would my sense of myself as an instrument of purpose-driven leadership and change continue to grow? I knew what my answers had to be as I encountered people who were trying to figure out the issues of life.

In Western society we've gotten all hung up on the management of conflict, hurt feelings, and the steadily available vortex of doom in the media and online. We spend a lot of energy reacting, avoiding, containing, blaming, getting partisan, scaring each other, feeling heated and helpless or ashamed and then usually exiting, getting quiet (or getting numb) instead of finding ways to do less catastrophizing and to be more connected and fruitful.

There are far more sophisticated biochemical explanations for the physical sensations and social consequences of all of this. But I think of emotion as having **two layers**. Both are useful in their own ways to our surviving and thriving; both are filled with somatic and social cues.

The **first layer** is instantly reactive and defensive. It's our early-warning physical and biochemical reaction to real and perceived danger. Our ancestors were inspired by the first layer to be ready to instantly assess, *Can I eat that?* And, *Can that eat me?* On the savannah, we didn't have the thickest skin or the biggest teeth or scariest claws, but we did, like all mammals, develop instantaneous reactivity. After all, "life has to win every day," while "death has to win just once." It makes sense that we see threats everywhere. We've been fighting, fleeing, and freezing for millennia. Perpetual crisis can be automatic! It's easy! And for some reason, we're just as easily spooked and negative now as we ever were—even in these amazing days of health, freedom, prosperity, and safety. We've got a "negativity bias," which can, of course, still protect us from lions, but it can also distort—and often become our easy and unexamined default. But when we slow down on the reactivity and discover that it's not really a lion, we breathe differently and move from reactivity to choice. What if it's really a pony?

And there's a **second layer of emotion. It's slower but just as adaptive.** Once we are secure enough to slow down and get to it, this layer helps us connect and communicate, be softer with each other, and create order. In the long run, the **second layer** became our species' greatest advantage. The **second layer** includes what I call **"belonging-longing."** And when we find consistent ways to inhabit the **second layer**, we get to connect and be courageous with challenges all at the same time. The **second layer** is where we can stand alone when we need to. The **second layer** is also where we can belong. The **second layer** is where we built civilizations that are not based simply on shared fears and hatreds. The **second layer** is where we are most alive.

Central to our work as coaches is growing clarity about our own two personal layers. What scares and annoys you? The most important thing is always what you will do next. The most obvious place for both layers to appear is with people we care about and work with.

If you're a parent, you've probably thought deeply about how to help your children learn about these layers of emotion. John and Julie Gottman at the University of Washington have observed and studied four ways of meeting a child who is experiencing big emotion.[29] Only one correlates to the best and most life-giving of outcomes.

Say a child's goldfish dies . . .

1. **Dismissing Behavior**. The parent says, "It's no big deal. We'll get another one." (Dismissing the child's feelings outright.)
2. **Disapproving Behavior**. It's a lot like dismissing, only the parent is also actively throwing stones at the child's reactions: "Grow up!" (Emotions are seen as weakness.)
3. **Laissez-faire**. The parent abdicates and doesn't engage at all, or shifts the focus to their own response story.
4. **Emotion coaching**. This is a combination of empathy (feeling with the child) and then helping the child to understand the nature of grief, and that it will go away and then come back, "kind of like when we stand with our toes in the surf." The parent is both accessible and responsive. It's no surprise that the fourth style yields the best childhood outcomes.

If you're like me, you've seen grown-up versions of each one of these approaches reflected in professional management styles.

Picture this . . .

I'm sitting down with a leader and her team of very clever, very busy people. We've met together before and share some trust. But today it's pretty quiet. I follow the energy and listen with my eyes to a roomful of **first layers**. Two people are staring at the floor and dodging eye contact. One guy wants to know if we're going to get all "woo-woo" today. One woman is leaning back, arms folded, looking surly. Another is asking how long we'll be meeting (she has important work to do). And another is getting all chirpy and asking who needs a seltzer. The leader is leaning in, looking in my direction. She knows that her team's subject matter expertise is not the issue. Something else is getting in the way. Everyone senses danger, and their physical presence reflects it.

I check my own reaction. Each of them looks overwhelmed in their own way. Am I? I already know that my personal **first-layer** response to the danger is to try to charm people. That won't help much. **Nor will it help if I . . .**

- *Start delivering tools and tips, telling, and fixing, or if I*
- *Ask each of them for their analysis of the issues (and who they think is to blame). This is a paradox because their big brains are responsible for much of their success. Except that, as a team, they're stuck, and their leading-edge ability to analyze doesn't seem to be helping.*
- *It won't help if I tell the surly one to leave and come back when she can be nice, at which time I'll teach her some communication skills, or if I*
- *Invite them to vent those powerful **first layers**.*

These people look sullen, reactive, angry, overwhelmed, helpless, hopeless, and scared. Venting that stuff will only make it worse. I am reminded of how instantly angry I can get in traffic when another driver does something unpredictable. I may look furious in the moment, but the truth is that I'm scared. Then as soon as I see an out-of-state license plate and a grateful wave from a disoriented visitor, my amygdala calms down, and I thank the **first-layer** reactivity for doing its job of preparing me to fight, fly, or freeze. Knowing I'm safe, I go back to my **second layer**, ready to return my attention to building civilization again.

Big emotion can sweep us all up.

I know (because they're mammals) that each member of this team wants to connect and belong, to be generous and receptive. If I can help them explore and get some access to their **second layers**, I know already that I'll hear things like:

- *"I'm scared I won't do this right."*
- *"I'm not really indifferent; I'm just frozen."*
- *"I'm worried I'll say the wrong thing."*
- *"I want you to trust that I'm trying."*
- *"This is foreign territory, and I don't know what to expect."*
- *"Maybe I'll fall apart or sound crazy or get hurt forever."*

Each person present—including the coach—comes with a story about (and good reasons for) their **first layer**.

Before I talk about what happened next . . .

Put yourself in my seat. What would your story be as the coach in the room? What are the sensations you notice? What are you automatically saying to yourself? How are you coaching yourself? How will you be able to return your attention to these good people and what they are offering you? For as long as you're a coach or coaching leader, you'll be getting better at paying attention in two directions: to your coachee, of course, but also to yourself. In your own reflective practices, self-awareness, and emotional regulation, you will become fluent in moving between the automatic **first layer** to the chosen **second layer**.

Take a moment and reflect on the following question (which I've asked myself repeatedly through the years):

"If a flag flew over the house you grew up in that announced to the world how your family dealt with big emotions (for example: rejection, sadness, conflict, grief, appreciation, attraction), what would have been written on it?"

I've also asked hundreds of people this question, and I've heard all kinds of answers:

- *"Be the boss. The person who stands up first wins."*
- *"Get invisible. Keep it to yourself."*
- *"Leave. Keep it to yourself."*
- *"Be silent and comply."*
- *"Defend yourself."*
- *"Yell. Get scary."*
- *"Be silent. Get scary."*
- *"Be perfect and blameless."*
- *"Breathe. Smile. And ask a question."*
- *"Do something funny."*
- *"Charm them."*
- *"Call Grandma."*
- *"Be extra nice and maybe hold hands."*
- *"Get busy fixing. Maybe go do the dishes."*
- *"Don't poke the bear."*
- *"Be the peacemaker. Find common ground."*
- *"Pout. Show everyone how hurt and offended you are."*
- *"Argue. Cite your source."*
- *"Let everyone know you're fine. Just fine."*
- *"Ask for everyone to pray about it with you."*
- *"There's no crying in baseball!"*

Those people who raised us usually got lots of things right. But when it comes to anger and resentment and shame and sadness and pain and loneliness and disagreeing and ambition and attraction and love, it's pretty common for families to have their own incomplete intergenerational patterns and stuck places. Now, as a grown-up, you likely find yourself responding in the same familiar (maybe **first layer**) way you always have. Habit has its own gravitational pull.

For example . . .

What would your response be if a coachee said in your sixth session, *"I'm not getting much out of our conversations. Can I get another Coach?"* **Here's a hint:** remember you are listening in two directions. Something historic in you probably gets bumped. Can you take a couple of breaths to coach yourself through "the automatic to the chosen"? And then can you return your attention to your coachee's experience?

When this happened to me a few years ago, I had to breathe through an instant **first-layer** cloud of hurt and shame and what-can-I-do-to-make-it-right?! And then I asked my coachee, *"How does it usually go for you when you're not getting what you want?"* Together, we challenged an old pattern in her life, and my coachee learned to speak up more for what she wanted. She didn't have to *"be silent and comply and just leave"* this time.

Your growing capacity for staying gently curious and collaborative with both layers of big emotion is right at the heart of your coaching presence. It makes you hugely interesting to human brains. Here's why. Psychologically and neurologically, when you get good at your own version of Level 3, your calm and unhurried presence gives the human brains with whom you engage a chance to join you in finding a new path through an old and familiar experience. And to maybe plant a new flag.

Back to my quiet, unhappy team . . .

I ask them to think about my flag question for a minute or two. Then I invite each person to tell a story, and gradually we begin to smile and laugh and become thoughtful together. I even catch glimpses of vulnerability. And bravery. We start to have a different experience. I stand beside them as they explore and name and get curious about each other's stories. They experience emotion as workable and even useful. They actually help each other out of that **first-layer vortex**.

Here's what I do that helps as I invite them to tell their stories . . .

- I **slow down** (**first-layer** reactivity is fast and automatic, and I want quiet amygdalae so that we can get to the unhurried **second layer—and to more trust**).
- I speak with **soft curiosity.** You can hold attention with your voice: *"Stay with me."*
- I keep things **simple and uncluttered.**
- I use their **words and stories.**
- I say what I see and hear (*"You just leaned in—seems like you don't want us to miss this."*).
- I help them create order—to see that emotion isn't irrational. Both layers are full of information.
- I remind myself that their stuckness isn't due to their lack of expertise; it's due to their process.

And then this happens . . .

Me [taking a breath and smiling]: *"OK. Who's got a story?"*

Surly Woman (SW) [emphatically]: *"I'll start. Our flag would have read, 'Make yourself useful.' When things got tense at the dinner table, I got good at finding something to fix."*

Me: *"You're still good at finding things to fix!"*

SW [smiling now]: *"Yes! And the bonus was that I could usually leave the drama at the table to go do it!"*

Me: *"So help me to see the picture: You're a normal kid. You just want to survive and belong. What early warning signals did you get physically that told you things were getting dramatic?"*

SW [getting quieter, beginning to use her second layer]: *"Hmm. I guess I'd start to hold my breath."*

Me [slowing down]: *"What would that mean?"*

SW: *"I don't know. That I'd better figure out how to be useful and go do it!"*

Me: *"So you held your breath, you got mad/scared/sad, you said to yourself, 'I'm going to go find something useful to do.' And you'd get to leave. Is that how it went?"*

SW [slowing down]: *"Well, yes."*

Me: *"This makes complete sense to me: As a kid you'd notice you were holding your breath as things got dramatic. That was your early warning signal to leave the table and "be useful."*

SW: *"And it was a bonus that I could get away from everyone's drama and go be useful **alone**!"*

A team member chimes in: *"You're still good at that too."*

[Everyone laughs.]

Me: *"Could you help me understand something else?"*

SW: *"OK."*

Me: *"As a kid, who had your back and helped you to breathe when things got dramatic?"*

SW: *[Shrugs]*

Team leader: *"Could I say something?"*
SW [*Rolls her eyes and smiles*]: *"OK."*
Team leader: *"Well. I could have your back here."*
SW [*Thoughtfully*]: *"I'm not sure I know what that would look like."*
Me: *"Thanks for going first."*

(Surly woman becomes visibly less surly and leans in to hear the next story. Trust was getting fast-tracked.)

The team listens as each one tells a story and allows me and their team members to respond. I stand beside them as they have an experience, de-escalate, make it safe enough, and find some order. They slow down and find that **second layer** that mammals love to live in. I walk around in it with them and help them keep their balance in the unevenness and to help each other. My continuous self-coaching is crucial. I help them experience the **second layer**. It's life-giving. And as they get access to it, the ROI of this time seems clear.

Every day these people see and work with each other, and now they are giving each other a new experience, maybe even a way out of an historic **first-layer** reaction that never really has worked very well. Who knew that so much personal growth and healing could happen at work?

It's true that coaching isn't therapy . . .

We're not diagnosing or prescribing or spending hours unraveling old hurt places or billing insurance companies. As coaches we invite people to glance at their historic patterns, stories, and strengths, but our gaze always returns to the present and the future. However, as with a great therapeutic relationship, a great coaching partnership touches our hearts and motivations and sense of purpose in the world in some deep ways. It's equally poignant. And when a coach invites, respects, engages with, and explores a coachee's emotional wisdom—without attachment to being right or fixing—the possibilities increase for the coachee's clear and sustainable movement through the stages of change.

Do you remember in the Key Skills when we talked about **using the bright spots and positively defining stories of the person or team you're coaching?** We've all got defining stories and historic patterns about how we first learned to survive and belong. Usually, those defining stories emerged as we paid attention to our reactive **first layers**. When a coach understands the power of slowing down, of being softly curious, and of speaking simply, they can invite their coachees to glance back at their defining stories and then to move their gaze to the present and to the reality they want to create going forward as they explore and use their **second layer** with people they care about and work with. It can be poignant.

As I drive away from the team meeting . . .

I get in the slow lane and do a little self-coaching. I've been ON for several hours, and great things have happened. Now I pay attention to my own thoughts and to my own breathing. I think about what I need to reflect on as I head home or to my next coaching interaction. The people in both places need me to be present, accessible, and responsive.

And I need me to be present! This is a big part of the deal—If I don't attend to my own practices of reflection and self-care and to staying connected to my own colleagues, I'll set myself up for resentment, diminished effectiveness, and maybe even burnout.

At the core of coaching presence is your ability to tolerate—even welcome and use—big emotions, both your own and those of the people you coach. So where are you with emotion? In your **first layer**, what scares you? What sends you into Level 1 listening?

Is it the message on your old flag?

Or is it a cause or something deep in your own experience or convictions? Maybe it's political or personal or something that's a raw place somewhere in your own healing. Maybe it's an issue in which you see no gray area. Coaches, like good reporters, cannot fairly make their work about those things.

Years ago, I worked with a politician whose policies, I thought, would lead to the end of civilization as we know it. "I can do this," I thought. "I'm a professional." But she kept touching a nerve in my life, and about five sessions into our work, I caught myself starting to offer suggestions about what the politician should be thinking about and working on. Ultimately, *because* I'm a professional, I was candid with her about what I had found myself beginning to do and why. We agreed together that a referral to another coach was a good idea, and we partnered to close our coaching relationship and to create a strong transition.

When this happens to you, and it will, turn to your tribe and consult. And if you need to, make a referral. This just means that you respect and care for your deeply held—or felt—personal convictions elsewhere in your life.

As we continue on, we'll be asking you to examine your own life, to glance at your historic patterns and to then gaze at your own **second layer**—the layer that helps you know you belong, that we need you, and that you are alive in the best of ways. When a coach can lead the way in being vulnerable, trust hits the fast track.

As a Cohort, we'll explore the application of all this to the growth of your coaching presence. Don't worry. In our upcoming sessions we're not going to freak you out; we'll just invite you to continue to test and learn, mostly with "10-percent shifts." As you build your life, and maybe your family, what do you want written on your current flag?

We're in your corner.

In the SeattleCoach Stash: *Listen to my four minutes on "If a Flag Flew Over the House You Grew Up In."*[5]

Your Coaching Presence

Finding Your Fluency

In any situation, the person who can most accurately describe reality without laying blame
will emerge as the leader, whether designated or not. —Edwin Friedman

There's an old Christian saying: "Preach the gospel at all times. When necessary, use words."
Maybe there's a corollary when it comes to excellent coaching presence: "Show up like a coach at all times.
When it helps to speak, speak. When it helps to be silent, be silent."

In our journey together, we've focused on the essential concrete practices of "doing coaching," and we've talked about how to coach "Big Emotions." And now, we've moved our emphasis to your coaching presence, to your ability to "be the coach." Our goal is to help you grow in your ability to be fully present and engaged, coaching yourself through your own assumptions, emotions, reflexive "defaults," sensations, and curiosity even as you coach another. Even though they are always reflecting, learning, aspiring, and growing, great coaches are also solidly grounded. They are contagious.

Excellent coaches and coaching leaders understand and cultivate their personal presence as their primary instrument. So, now I have another question about one of your "defaults."

Which corner in the diagram (northwest or southeast) feels easiest and most natural to you? Both are strengths. (Your friends probably know.)

Challenging comes easy
for you. You are truthful
and direct.
"Clear is kind!"

Being supportive comes easy
for you. You are a
compassionate cheerleader.
"Be gracious! Everyone is
fighting a hard battle."

Think of finding fluency as a coach or coaching leader as the practice of getting access to the next most useful thing to say or do: the most useful question, observation or comment, spoken in the right moment, in the right manner, and with the most generative outcomes in mind. Maybe it's unhurried and thoughtful. Maybe it's a blurt. Maybe it's from the strength you just thought of. Maybe it requires something from the other corner.

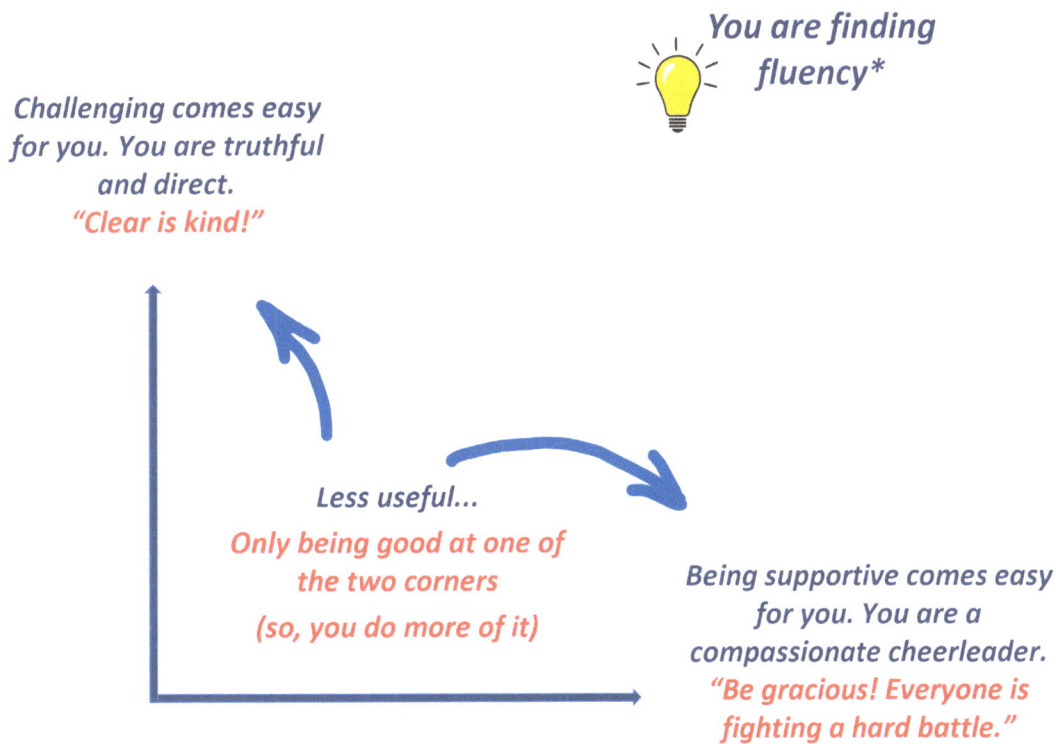

*You are finding fluency**

Challenging comes easy for you. You are truthful and direct.
"Clear is kind!"

Less useful...
Only being good at one of the two corners
(so, you do more of it)

Being supportive comes easy for you. You are a compassionate cheerleader.
"Be gracious! Everyone is fighting a hard battle."

Here's another question: *If you were to experiment with a 10-percent shift from your default strengths toward the fluency lightbulb, what would you try? What beliefs would you have to challenge?*

In Family Systems Theory, your understanding and access to the lightbulb corner is a feature of **differentiation.** And it's contagious in the best of ways. It's the cornerstone of systemic intelligence. This is any leader's most effective personal "home base": You are calm, non-anxious, unhurried, and authoritative. You've got access to the **second layer** of emotion we were just talking about. You know how to listen to explore and how to listen to respond, balancing inquiry and advocacy. You know how to both stand alone and to belong. Without self-preoccupation, you know how to listen to your own life too.

As a differentiated leader, you can say what needs to be said (like the stuff everyone in the room already senses) without blaming. You coach the person more than the problem. You use what my friend Peggy Gilmer (who sometimes coaches with an assist from her horses) calls **"minimum essential influence"**; i.e., *"Tough as I need to be and as soft as I can be."*

- Differentiation means you can be a separate "**I**" while remaining connected.
- When things go sideways, humans tend to look for a scapegoat—someone to blame. Differentiated people are open to the possibility that they are a participant in the drama triangles around them

(and not just an aggrieved victim). They stay engaged (rather than "cutting off") and can be less automatic and anxious. They coach themselves to be more voluntary and intentional.

- Leaders who work on their own self-differentiation challenge their followers to do the same.
- Differentiated systems are better able to stay connected in times of pressure and disagreement and to engage in support and challenge that is timely, specific, respectful, and future-oriented.
- And differentiated leaders are able to embrace their "belonging-longing" as they see the role of other people in bringing more life and awareness.

Great coaching leaders—even if they're not positional leaders—grow steadily in their emotional intelligence, in their social intelligence and influence, and in their understanding of how human systems work.

Note: Once you have completed "Coaching for Leaders," we'll invite you to continue with us in advanced consultation cohorts, where we'll focus even more on your personal systemic intelligence with individuals, groups, and teams. As you navigate those complex processes and relationships, we'll continue to talk about how to build alliance, agreement, and agenda—and how to honor confidentiality in each of those settings.

When Coaching Presence Wins: A SeattleCoach Case Study

What would you do when you ask a coachee, *"What do you want to work on?"* and they just do not have a ready answer—but you know they are coachable? That was SeattleCoach Kim Jarvis's experience. And with her permission, this is the note back to her from a very satisfied coachee:

> *Kim Jarvis is my coach, and it is my distinct pleasure to give her my highest recommendation. Kim has not only enriched my professional life, she has also enriched my personal life.*
>
> *Our work together was complex; in the sense that the goals I had set for myself were truly uncharted and complicated by interpersonal challenges with key individuals that would be critical in the achievement of my goals. I needed someone who could take all the facets of my undefined plan and make sense of the whole mess.*
>
> *Kim was able to see my struggles and provide just the right mix of insight and guidance to allow me to celebrate my own conclusions. In her line of work, I can see it being a MUCH faster process to provide the answers, but as a recipient of her professional and caring coach approach I am glad she invested in MY process rather than focusing on quick wins. I had to work for my victories and realizations which made them meaningful and actionable.*

In the SeattleCoach Stash: *Listen to my three minutes on Coaching Presence.*[t]

And a few of my favorite books *on the subject of Systems Theory.*[30]

Giving Feedback Like a Coach

Real Life and the Impact of The Rule of Four

Psychotherapy helps you get rid of neurotic (i.e., habitual, automatic, irrational) misery so that you can use your strength to fight ordinary misery (i.e., the relentless challenges of life). —Patty's paraphrase of Freud's epiphany

Since around 2001 at the University of Pennsylvania, researchers have been studying a phenomenon that has been in plain sight for millennia—that human brains find it easier to criticize, blame, and look for the grim than to see the virtuous, the good, and the overall positive trend line. We have a "negativity bias" that has helped us survive, but it also makes us hardwired to focus on the dismal, the discriminatory, and disconnected—even though we live in amazing times and are surrounded by other humans, most of whom are trying their best most of the time every day.

We are also hardwired to connect.

The researchers began with a question: *We have a manual for categorizing and diagnosing human psychiatric pathology (*The Diagnostic and Statistical Manual of Mental Disorders*); what if we developed a categorization of human virtues? That is, virtues that are honored and cultivated worldwide?*

And more recently, they turned their attention to the question of what it would take for human brains to challenge and counteract our deeply ingrained "negativity bias." Interestingly, this research has coincided with the explosive growth of professional coaching.

The consistent finding (I've noted several references and resources at https://www.seattlecoach.com/seattlecoach-cfl-the-stash.html) has been **The Rule of Four**: it generally takes a steady pattern of four "positives" in order for a human brain to grow enough trust and confidence over time to effectively face the less frequent, and sometimes necessary, "negatives."

Life is tough. And life is a relentless teacher. Our hearts get broken. We fail. We suck at stuff. We become ex's and victims, and sometimes we hurt other people. Sometimes we must protect ourselves. The challenges and resistance we get in the course of life, both internally and externally, are part of the deal. Think of those relentless challenges, emotions, and obstacles that life brings as the negatives. In our own lives and in our work as coaches and leaders, the goal can never be the elimination of ordinary misery. The goal cannot realistically be the elimination of risk or the embrace of chronic grievances, nor can it be the creation of life-long emotional warning labels and dependency. In addition, there is no human emotion or obstacle that can be forever shunned or pathologized or avoided.

We've all experienced the **first layer** of Big Emotion, where our automatic response to conflict or misunderstanding is fear, anger, shame, or discouragement. Reactivity and grace rarely go together. And rebalancing that 1:1 ratio isn't easy. **The Rule of Four** is different from the (usually) uninvited "feedback sandwich" ("praise-correction-praise," which everyone hates) that many of us were trained to deliver.

The Rule of Four

For years I rowed competitively, mostly in the big "eights" you see on Lake Union and Lake Washington. It is a beautiful sport that, done well, is full of metaphors. Here is one of my favorites: It is resistance against a rower's oar that drives a racing shell forward—but only if she gets the ratio right. The rhythm must be a minimum of a 4:1 ratio between a skilled and balanced recovery (the smooth glide that happens when the blades are out of the water and swinging back for the next "catch") and the connected, explosive, and muscular "drive" that begins when the rowers "catch" the water in unison and pull against the resistance of the water. In rowing and in life, 5:1 glide to resistance/challenge is even better.

Every rowing coach knows this: when glide blends with resistance/challenge in a lesser ratio of 2:1 or 1:1, learning and accomplishment—like a racing shell—slow down. It may look full of effort, but it is not efficient. And it is not fast.

If you have ever been in a relationship where people mostly listen to respond rather than listen to understand, you know that their conversations might sound splashy and energetic, but connection and movement rarely happen. There is not much glide.

When people live with chronic stress, their bodies respond with the same physiological and behavioral readiness (heart rate, sweat glands, shallow breathing) as a person facing a life-and-death scenario. The demanding leader barks, *"I want you at that meeting,"* and the team member reacts involuntarily from the same state as a human facing a predator (fight: *"Again?!"* Or flight: Looking down at their phone, *"I'll try to be there."*). And safety and trust, collaboration and learning diminish in both people.

Chronic vigilance is just as harmful as acute vigilance is beneficial (like the clear direction you shout in an emergency). And both are contagious. The problem with chronic vigilance is that learning, connection, kindness, and creativity become less possible. One of our coaches wondered if there might be a correlation between chronic vigilance "and stupid." Hmm. Maybe.

My favorite rabbi, mentor, and thought-leader, the late Edwin Friedman, had this to say about trust: ***"Others can only hear you when they are moving toward you, no matter how eloquently you phrase the message. In other words, as long as you are in the pursuing, rescuing, or coercive position, your message, no matter how eloquently broadcast, will never catch up."***[31]

Here's a bottom line: our brains have no trouble looking for the negative. That's the easiest and most automatic thing they do.

A relentless focus on inadequacy and blame may create a reaction, but it doesn't help us learn or form deep bonds or take calculated risks. When we instead give attention to strengths and aspirations, to creative initiatives, we catalyze learning, creativity, connection—and even belonging (remember **belonging-longing**?). That, of course, takes practice and discipline and attention to team culture as we shift our resources and sense of reality to gratitude, opportunity, and possibility.

Our core job as coaches is to master ways of creating both the conditions and the behaviors required for more trust, engagement, openness, calm, and thus, learning. When we do that, we set the stage for Level 3 conversations. If we are safe as well as compelling and challenging, the people we coach are biochemically able to deepen their resilience, gratitude, perspective, compassion, and self-efficacy. These are the conditions that foster hope and "neuroplasticity" that happens throughout life.

As coaches and leaders, we train much of our attention on our coachee's strengths, virtues, possibilities, learning, connections, effort, resilience, and positive stories. Again, it is never that we ignore obstacles, fears, past injuries, growing edges, performance gaps, and structural challenges (remember, life is relentless). It is just a matter of focus and leverage. Again, the negatives might wake us up and challenge us, but the positives make sustainable change possible.

What The Rule of Four Looks Like in Practice

At this point in your life, you've learned some things about how to weather storms. You're not chronically offended. You don't scare easily. You know that healthy emotional immunity stands up well to sorrow and adversity. You're resilient, and, as a friend of mine says, "You're probably either up or getting up." You've got a big heart, but you also know that trying to offer too much empathy (aka rescuing, commandeering, propping up, or fixing) can result in what one presidential speech writer called "the soft bigotry of low expectations." Maybe you're learning that compassion, like that separate-and-connected warm handshake, is better.

You have some idea about what is changeable in your temperament. And you have made peace with some things too.

When we got underway with **CFL**, I asked you to take **The VIA Character Strengths Survey**, an assessment designed to help people identify, develop, and then use their best character qualities in pursuit of their goals. One key finding in this on-going research is that a "capitalization model," which focuses on strengths, is superior in important ways to a "compensation model," which focuses on remediating deficiencies.

Maybe you have a spiritual practice, a faith, or a belief in an intelligent, affectionate creator. This is not required for a happy life, but it seems to bring an additional advantage—one that sharpens your focus on the pursuit of goodness and wholeness. But there's a big "if." It's the part about the creator in your faith being affectionate, even interested, in the course of your brief time on the planet.

Remember the **Key Skills** of "leveraging the coachee's values, strengths, energy" of "using their bright spots and defining stories"? Having answers to some of the following questions might help with refining your own ratio:

- *What have you noticed about your way of earning trust and allowing others to know you better?*
- *What do you know about how you "land" your personal expressions of gratitude, kindness, and respect?*
- *How do people know when you are paying attention to them?*
- *What happens when people know you have truly forgiven them?*
- *How do people know when something is hugely important to you?*
- *Who is in your corner? (And, maybe a funny question, Do they know how much they mean to you?)*
- *What is your process of making important decisions?*
- *When and how do you know you need to step back, reflect, process and recharge, and then return to a conversation?*

Again, your answers to these questions are most likely to show up over time rather than in single conversations. And that's good news for us lifelong course-correctors who are sometimes inelegant, impatient, and self-centered and need forgiveness and reconnection.

Coaches are masters at exploring what works, maybe what has always worked in safe-enough human systems and societies. And whatever your temperament or background, you already know some of the behaviors that work best given how we humans are wired. Teams that work together toward operating at Level 3 find ways to get better at

- *Continuing to breathe, recover, and reset in the face of difficult emotions.*
- *Helping each member explore his or her own personal way of doing those things.*
- *Quickly noticing resistance, disagreement, even the need to create a boundary.*
- *Staying connected and curious, inviting more conversation about others' underlying assumptions and experiences.*
- *Helping members to learn the warm handshake—to be separate and connected at the same time.*
- *Inviting more collegial intelligence into shared work.*
- *When necessary, apologizing, reconnecting, and repairing damage.*

Leaders and teams that cultivate a positive rhythm of glide to resistance/challenge in the work and structure of their teams foster systems that course-correct and learn. Their systems are also both contagious and attractive.

In human systems, something is always "catching," and we get to decide what that is.

Life itself brings more than enough resistance and challenge to each of us. Start with kindness as you help your coachee face it.

In the SeattleCoach Stash: *Listen to my three minutes about "The Rule of Four."*[u]

And in the SeattleCoach Stash PDF: *My favorite resources about positivity.*[32]

Giving Feedback Like a Coach

Refining the "How-to"

If you're not in the arena, also getting your ass kicked, I'm not interested in your feedback. —Brené Brown

As we've mentioned, "feedback" has become one of the most dreaded of words. Whether you are offering or receiving "feedback," it can be an unhappy proposition. Again, many of the professionals I have worked with have been trained to deliver the (usually) uninvited "bleep" sandwich ("praise-correction-praise," which obviously violates The Rule of Four).

Throughout our time together, we've talked about feedback that works in the context of strong relationships. As we've grown in our alliances, we've used great feedback to strengthen your understanding and practice of

- The Core Four (respect, energy, acknowledgment, listening)
- The power of knowing how to "Coach Big Emotions"
- Clarity about the power of your coaching presence and about its application over time of
- The Rule of Four (instead of the "feedback sandwich")

And we're just getting started!

When couples, friends, colleagues, and teams make it a point to build and bank strengths and assets in a challenging environment, they connect and learn better and more sustainably. Human brains must be psychologically safe-enough in order to sustainably learn from each other. Not bubble-wrapped. Just safe enough to be coachable. (Remember? "Open to insight. Open to try stuff.")

Feedback that works draws from a bank of trust that grows over time, and as we make regular deposits, it is increasingly possible to constructively talk about the rough spots with each other. The rough stuff might wake us up, but it is our deliberate, habitual orientation to strengths, virtue, possibilities, support, opportunities, course-corrections, wise risk-assessment, and connection that make recovery and learning sustainable.

Recently, I was listening to a business owner—a good coaching leader—as he provided some timely course-correction to a valued member of his organization, a customer-facing team leader. Both of them agreed to have me present as the coaching leader expressed this private correction:

Biz owner: *"I know you care about doing the job right; you just have this one little thing." [He smiles and his voice gets soft.]*
Customer-facing team leader (CFTL) *[looking sheepish]: "My cursing?"*
Biz owner: *"Yeah."*
CFTL: *"That's just how I am. The people I hang out with, that's just how we talk. That's just how we are."*
Biz owner *[listening]: "I want you to change your behavior." [He pauses, **CFTL** listens and nods.] "I'm very protective of (the business's) image. The last thing I want is for people to think we're all about profanity. Would that be good for business?"*
CFTL: *"Possibly not, and that's something I could work on."*
Biz owner *[pausing and smiling]: "Good to hear."*
CFTL: *[laughs easily]*

Biz owner, returning to the larger agenda: *"OK. We were talking about the performance system I've created . . ."*

Looks easy, doesn't it? But these two had a lot of trust in the bank. Did you notice? This business owner had a hunch that CFTL already knew what he was going to bring up. He did not begin with that usually mistaken belief that *"I know, and you don't."*

Drama and hard feelings diminish when there is good connection and ongoing communication over time. With these two, I did not see very much high blood pressure in the room. The biz owner used himself, his values, and the trust that he had cultivated with CFTL as he described his personal response to her behavior. Then he spoke the truth directly and made a request. CFTL sensed his respect and directness and responded to it far better, I thought, than if he had become indirect or simply demanded that CFTL comply with "the rules."

Respectful directness within a trusting relationship, even when it is tough, invites people to evaluate what is possible and desirable in making things better.

It is common sense: When people who are living in safe-enough conditions cultivate a habit of behaving in a voluntarily calm and connected way, mostly practicing **The Rule of Four**, relationships do better. And, by the way, at work, where we spend most of our adult waking hours, there is a clear ROI when a high-performance team identifies and commits to positive behaviors that are clear and measurable, frequent, and steady. Especially in the times when situational conflict becomes intense.

When I work with teams to establish rules of engagement, I usually assume that I will encounter some Big Emotion. So, I encourage everyone to **slow down** (remember, **first-layer** reactivity is fast, and I want quiet amygdalae so that we can get to the **second layer**), to speak with **soft curiosity,** and to keep things **simple and uncluttered.**

These are the SeattleCoach hallmarks I teach for practicing generative feedback with individuals:

1. You speak from calm authority, from your authentic grace-and-truth coaching presence, using yourself, your questions and statements of impact and being open to learning and being influenced.
2. If you need to, you give yourself time to calm down. Once your calm authority has returned, you speak as closely as possible to the "event" or observation. It is rarely useful to save up reactions for the next one-on-one or annual review.
3. You speak with curiosity and specifics to what is repeatable, changeable, and/or growing (a 10-percent shift?).
4. Over time, your Level 3 communication builds trust and reflects a focus on strengths.
5. You speak to the values and outcomes your coachee/employee identifies. Maybe with an eye toward your shared deliverables. Great coaches remember that everyone's version of "excellent" is a little bit idiosyncratic.
6. You speak the good stuff publicly and the tough stuff privately, and with permission.
7. And, of course, you speak with respect. And, unless the house is on fire, you are unhurried.

I recently joined a business owner and the rest of his team for an offsite where they hammered out and committed together to a few things they knew would strengthen their work together. Interestingly, many of those things were related to their meeting strategy. Here is what they came up with:

- *Devices off, beginning five minutes before we start so we have to look at each other instead;*
- *When we're together we get out-loud about the stuff we've done that took extra character and effort—our own and each other's;*

- *And when we get out-loud about the hard stuff—our disagreements, where we need help—we slow down a little, working at staying engaged, curious, and pragmatic;*
- *We'll in some way ask "permission" before giving advice;*
- *We'll work on balancing advocacy with inquiry—and congratulate ourselves when we do better;*
- *We'll show each other the respect of responding to messages within twenty-four hours;*
- *And all of us will be in charge of keeping our promises.*

This leader and his team know that the challenges of their shared work are unremitting and that deploying ideas like these will boost their ability to connect, to collaborate, to stay curious and compassionate—and to improve their business outcomes.

In the SeattleCoach Stash: *Listen to my three minutes on "Giving Feedback Like a Coach."*[v]

And in the SeattleCoach Stash PDF: *Two resources that are helping me to rehabilitate the word "Feedback."*[33]

A Personal-Vision Exercise

In 1963 Reverend King did not say, "I have an idea."

Self-efficacy, hope, optimism, and resilience are, of course, at the heart of our work. When you are truly hopeful, you have a sense of agency *("I bet I can do this!")*, and you also have a clear sense of what "this" is. Your values and strengths and aspirations grow clear—along with your path forward.

When a coach, or their coachee, quietly and thoughtfully reflects on their best hopes, details are likely to emerge. What do you glimpse on the horizon? Maybe you sense a gravitational pull toward something that could be life-giving. Think of visioning as a longer version of "meta-view."

This is not hypnosis. It's not woo-woo. It's simply an opportunity to bring all your ways of knowing into focus. We won't give you a script, but these are a few things to consider:

1. Start by asking the individual or the team what they've experienced and explored in this kind of reflecting. Clarify that this isn't hypnosis. You're not going to suggest things to them.
2. Explain what you'll do. *("This will take about 20 minutes. Put your stuff on the floor; you can keep your eyes open or not; sit so that your core is supporting you and you're giving your lungs lots of room to do their work . . .")* When you give clear direction to any exercise in coaching, people will trust you more, and their ability to learn and engage will increase.
3. Invite people to think about engaging all their intelligence, their memory, and imagination and physical sensations. Give them time to take a deep breath or two.
4. Ask people to set their own "horizon." Let them know that this could be a few weeks to several months.
5. Then talk them through imagining a satisfying day "out there." Be gently curious with them: ***"What's going on as you begin to move through the day? What do you see on your calendar? Who's thanking you? And for what? Whom are you thanking? And for what?"*** Take your time. Let silence do the work.
6. At the close of the exercise, take a few unhurried minutes and invite people to write down their impressions and keepers—anything that felt deeply important or resonant.

Then invite some voluntary debriefing:

- *"What was it like as you looked into the future?" (restlessness, excitement, unease, joy . . .)*
- *"What did you see? Who was around? Anything about your physical environment?"*
- *"What were the obstacles? The opportunities?"*
- *"Who was thanking you? And for what, specifically?"*
- *"Whom were you thanking? And for what, specifically?"*

It's true, Reverend King is famous for telling a crowd of thousands who were gathered with him at the Lincoln Memorial in 1963 that he "had a dream."[34] It seems that his dream was a "tractor beam" for his life, and millions of us ended up sharing his dream. Maybe this exercise will help connect you to your own dream—to the things that are becoming most desirable and even possible in your work as a coach or coaching leader.

Your Next Steps/Personal Vision and Version Exercise

Do you remember what it was like when you set out on this journey? Maybe you were skeptical, or excited, or worried that you wouldn't get it all exactly right. But still you set out, testing and learning and deepening the heart of your leadership. Each step has taken courage, curiosity, and connection.

Now, as we move into "the end of the beginning," we'll ask you to take some to reflect both on where you've been and on where you're headed as a coaching leader. Then we'll invite you to share a snapshot of some potential next steps, not only for you but also for your impact. What could things look like for you six to eighteen months from now?

We have asked you about how and where you like to work, about how you personally establish **alliance, agreement, and agenda** with the people you lead and coach. We have talked about your personal coaching presence. You have begun to find hunches about how your path as a coaching leader will not only build your personal effectiveness but also likely contribute to meaningful growth in the people and teams you influence, and to the emerging growth mindset of both your career and your culture.

The purpose of the Next-Steps Exercise is for you to speak thoughtfully to other members of our Coaching for Leaders Cohort for around five minutes about how you are making this work your own, how you are talking about it, and what you think you would like to aspire to next. Think of this as a thoughtful personal review of how things stand for you here at the threshold of your next chapter.

In our sessions, we will ask you to talk with us about how you will continue and deepen your leadership coaching skills and presence. As your colleagues, we will listen and appreciate at Level 3.

Some ideas on how to prepare . . .

I.   Start by "interviewing" yourself: Where do things stand for you today?

As a member of this Cohort, you have spent most of a year taking in new ideas, testing-and-learning, sorting, customizing, and curating. We have challenged you to experience yourself as a coach.

1. *"How have you changed? What has grown deeper? What are you leaving behind?"*
2. *"What are you proudest of in your development as a coach?"*
3. *"What are the things that have especially influenced you from your reading and practice as you have been engaged in this process? Any key books, websites, thought leaders?"*
4. *"What have you learned about how you like to work?"*
   a. Regarding the people you want to serve: *"What are their challenges? What are they struggling with? What percentage of them will actually invest time and/or money in finding solutions or achieving specific outcomes? What is their vocabulary?"*
   b. *"What is the extra 'value-add' or personal interest or subject matter expertise you want to bring to your coaching?"* (For example: health and fitness, leaders and their teams, spiritual direction, career development, communication, managing disagreement, transitions, parenting, families with aging parents, . . .)

5. *"Currently, what are your biggest concerns? Obstacles to overcome?"*
6. *"What have you learned from your interviews with veteran coaching leaders that you are paying attention to?* (see below)
7. *"What are some of your key words?"*
8. *"What are you increasingly excited about in the development of your coaching leadership?"*
9. *"How are your bringing your leadership coaching wisdom to your subject matter expertise?"*
10. *"What are your best hopes for the coming months?"*

II.   Next, find and interview some veteran coaches or coaching leaders to have a conversation with.

The idea is to find experienced coaching leaders who work in a way you admire and would like to know more about. They can be local or not, well-known, or not, internal, or maybe an external coach that you trust. See if you can get a 15-minute interview with one or more of these great people. You can review our long list of graduates at www.SeattleCoach.com.[x] Each one would be happy to talk with you (they had to do this too!). Here are some potential questions. Mark the ones that look interesting to you:

1. *"Where did your passion for coaching originate?"*
2. *"What is the meaning you see in your work?"*
3. *"How do you factor coaching into your leadership style? Into your SME?"*
4. *"How have you built your brand and influence as a coach inside of your organization?"*
5. *"What are some of the mistakes you've made along the way that would help me to know about?"*
6. *"What do you think the emerging growth-mindset culture of your company needs more of from coaching leaders like you?"*
7. *"What are a few of your non-negotiable best practices?"*

Following your interviews, summarize a few takeaways that you believe will be helpful to you.

III.   Then think about how you want to talk about all of this.

What is the core of your message right now? Of your brand? In your **Next-Steps/Personal Vision and Version Exercise** tell us about it in a way that's congruent with your energy. Maybe what you say to us will be the message you repeat and build on in your writing, speaking, and leading.

Maybe you'll include things like:

1. *Your hopes for yourself*
2. *Your hopes for this organization*
3. *What, specifically, you hope to do to continue growing in your coaching skill and presence in the coming three to six months?*
4. *Who will know?*

IV.   Raise your bar.

The challenge with this exercise is to create the learning, support, and accountability that will be most meaningful to you—and most aligned with your emerging personal vision. Through the years, coaches have presented with the help of decks, essays, poetry, and even their personal "walk-on" music.

Whatever means you choose to use, as your colleagues, we will listen and appreciate at Level 3.

- *"If there is something you would like specific feedback on, tell us."*
- *"Tell us about your 'takeaways' from your conversations with those veteran coaches."*
- *"Improve your presenting skills—make your content 'sticky.'"*
- *"Set things up to get specific responses from us,*
- *And tell us your plan for continuing to build into the lives of other coaching leaders—and to invite them to build into your own. It is hard to be a great and ethical coaching leader without a tribe (also, it is way less fun)."*

And bonus points if you develop something you could use in the future as you help build a coaching culture.

V.   We'll give you feedback like coaches.

With your permission, we will then spend about 10 minutes with you, using the trust we have "in the bank," to share our statements of impact and probably a few questions that may help you "go down a layer" in your thinking. We will support you and acknowledge your courage and creativity throughout our time in CFL and specifically in this moment. As coaches giving feedback,

- *We will be specific*
- *And unhurried (but "close to the event").*
- *We will speak to what you bring up that we see getting deeper and stronger in your life and work. Maybe we will share our observations about how we have seen you expand your coaching skills and presence.*
- *We'll probably be supportive–and may ask for your permission to be direct.*
- *And we will speak from our own calm coaching presence.*

And, as we give feedback like coaches, we will keep the spotlight on you and your thinking and on any specific feedback you ask us for. What this means is that, in this time, even if we get excited about what you present, we won't start giving you advice or adding to what we think you should do next. We'll coach.

VI.   And remember, "SeattleCoach is a professional development program that leaves a community of allies in its wake." Tell us your plan for staying connected with other coaching leaders.

How will you tap into the tribe of which you are now a key part? How will you create regular time for mutual support and learning as you continue to grow? Members of earlier CFL Cohorts have

1. Continued to meet informally or for peer coaching;
2. Joined one of our professional certification Cohorts;[y]
3. Or volunteered to be a Triad Coach with future CFL Cohorts in their organization.

Breathe. This will be fun. Remember, **hope is a combination of vision + self-efficacy, and it is powerful**. (Plus you know we have your back, right?)

Finally, through our months together you have heard some of our coaches tell their **One Coach's Story**. We want you to be able to do that too. The following article, "Your 'One Coach's Story,'" may be useful to you.

In the SeattleCoach Stash: *Listen to my five minutes on the purpose of these "Next Steps Exercise."*[z]

Your "One Coach's Story"

Only experience can make [wisdom] a visceral part of our daily lives by bridging the distance from head to heart.
That's why a storyteller is magic, but a teller of facts is not. There is a reason why parables are the oldest form
of teaching: they work. — Gloria Steinem, *Revolution from Within: A Book of Self-Esteem*

Have You Noticed?

At SeattleCoach we keep asking you to mine your experiences and explore your life, even your sense of calling, and then to be able to talk about why you see yourself as a coach or coaching leader: *What makes you unique? How do you like to work? Whom do you want to serve?"*

And you should know that we have a tradition: every time our larger SeattleCoach tribe comes together, someone tells their "One Coach's Story." The volunteer stands up, and in about five minutes talks about their journey to this moment, and to this growing craft, in their life. This, of course, is practice for speaking to everyone in the rest of your personal and professional life.

We are at a time in history when the price of data, facts, and figures is falling—they are available everywhere. What is not falling is our delight in listening to a compelling story—a story that may connect some dots and, along the way, teach, protect, inspire, or delight us and our listeners. In an evolutionary way, we are all creators and consumers of comedies, dramas, and love stories. We even make up stories in our sleep.

And for a coaching leader, storytelling is an essential skill as we explain, truth-tell, persuade, and encourage.

Writing Your Story

What do you know about the nature of a good story? Here is the oldest of story lines: ***an ordinary person goes on a quest.*** And those ordinary people are usually vulnerable and flawed heroes (Odysseus, Precious Ramotswe, Frodo, Katniss Everdeen, Harry Potter, Ellen Ripley). When the great teacher Moses received his call to lead, he worried, "O Lord, I'm not very good with words. I never have been, and I am not now, even though you have spoken to me. I get tongue-tied, and my words get tangled" (Ex 4:10, NLT).

Don't you love a great story? We listen, we empathize and recognize, and we breathe in lessons. And maybe we wonder, *Maybe I could go on a quest too.*

As Usual, We Do Not Have a Formula for Writing Your Story

But we do have a few questions for you:

- What personal experience moved you into this journey toward coaching leadership? *Restlessness? Wondering, "Is this it?!" A slow dawning? Getting older? A loss? Your sense of purpose + mortality?* What happened? Who believed in you?

- And then what happened? What did you do? What were your inquiries and experiments, and what did you begin to notice? How did your direction come into focus as you moved through contemplation to preparation to action? Do you remember the first time you identified yourself as a coach or coaching leader?

- Like most of us with a learner's mind, you probably had times when you felt like a vulnerable beginner. What happened when you allowed people to see that you were new at this?

- What did you do when it began to seem too hard, even impossible? When you encountered significant internal or external resistance and, like Moses, you just wanted to give up and "go back to Egypt?"

- And when you kept learning and kept going, how did you refine your core message? How did you continue to talk about your emerging craft and presence as a coaching leader? And to whom? And then whom? Was there a point of no return?

- What convictions and core truths began to become confirmed in your heart? Who began to notice? What hard data and research and science aligned with and fortified your message?

- And, as your message about the value of coaching has begun to connect with the people you increasingly want to influence and serve, what are you contemplating? What might you do next?

Since the beginning of coach training, we have been asking you to identify the elements of your story and to test-drive them with both the members of this Cohort and supportive colleagues who are following your coaching journey.

In the years to come, as you keep re-telling and refining the story of your journey into coaching leadership, who knows? The next time the whole SeattleCoach tribe comes together, we may ask you to stand and deliver your *"One Coach's Story."*

In the SeattleCoach Stash PDF: Two of my favorite books about telling your story.[35]

Welcome to the End of the Beginning!

Now this is not the end. It is not even the beginning of the end. But it is, perhaps, the end of the beginning. — Winston Churchill, 1942, after a long-awaited victory

Hey Coach! You did it! For the last several months, I have seen you shine in the things that matter most:

- In your integrity
- In your seriousness and in your playfulness
- In your thoughtfulness
- In your uniqueness and
- In your relentless desire to get good at the words and music of leading like a coach

You've earned our deep respect and a place in our hearts, and it's a privilege for us to know you as colleagues. You've earned your **CFL Badge** to use in your web presence, LinkedIn profile, and with your signature. On the SeattleCoach website,[aa] I tell the world what you've just accomplished.

Staying in touch and tuned-up

1. I invite everyone who has trained with **SeattleCoach** to post quotes, stories, resources, events, opportunities, requests, and learnings on our private Facebook (FB) Group page. Just type "SeattleCoach" in your FB search box, click on the "group," and we'll approve your membership asap. We'll also keep all the latest news posted on our **SeattleCoach Network LinkedIn Group.**[bb]
2. Remember, I post new resources first in the **SeattleCoach Newsletter, "Coachable!"**[cc]
3. And you're invited to our monthly virtual **Happy Hour:**[dd] First Tuesdays. Fun. Free. Fascinating. Four o'clock (PT). Forty-five minutes.
4. And at our annual "**Coachtoberfest!"**[ee] (*"Reunions of people you can't wait to meet."*).
5. If the day comes when you'd like to become certified as a professional coach, be in touch and we'll usher you into one of our professional credentialing *"Flagship Cohorts."*[ff]

My greatest hope for you as you continue to "do the craft and be the coach" is that you apply to your own life everything you know about coaching, ensuring that you are happy in your work, intentional about your circle of colleagues, and finding your relationships with your family and friends to be your most enduring source of happiness. Thanks for all you've just done—and will do—to enrich the lives around you. You've enriched mine.

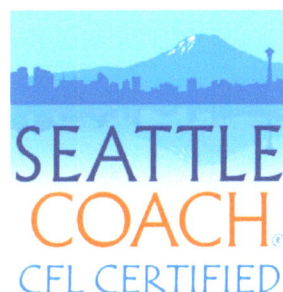

To the Journey Then,

Appendix

Appendix: Article I

What Happens When Your
Leaders Learn to Coach?

In the spring of 2008, Patty Burgin began to train small cohorts of mid-career professionals. In their own ways, each person had asked her some version of, "How do I learn to do what you do?" And each person was seeking certification in this emerging old/new profession of coaching. That same year SeattleCoach became a credentialed training provider of the International Coaching Federation (ICF). Since then, hundreds of SeattleCoaches have pursued the rigorous preparation required for professional certification. These small cohorts of allies have become known as SeattleCoach Flagship Cohorts.[gg]

Then in 2015, leaders and their organizations began to ask us for executive coaching education for their veteran leaders. This track could be briefer and more customized. We listened and began to understand that this second wave would require three things:

1. *Sponsoring executives who understood the value of coaching,*
2. *Leaders and people-managers who were raising their hands, and*
3. *External executive coaches who knew how to facilitate and model the learning.*

In response, we co-created rich cohort experiences for organizational leaders and their teams. Rather than focusing on professional credentialing, these veteran leaders and their sponsors are aiming to increase their leadership effectiveness. They too are SeattleCoaches. And they are building world-class coaching cultures. We called this second wave, Coaching for Leaders (CFL).[hh]

Happily, in the years since 2008, approximately half of the hundreds of coaches we've trained at SeattleCoach have become entrepreneurial, credentialed coaches. Since 2015, and the development of CFL, just as many have stayed in place in great companies and organizations—only now, as better bosses and people managers.

Coaching is a twenty-first-century leadership movement. Organizations that are succeeding in the twenty-first century have leaders who are both empathic and agile—with their markets and with their talent. Jobs, careers, and teams are changing. What is not changing is the fact that people who find ways to work well together (and with their screens) are more likely to, as we say at SeattleCoach, *make money, have fun, and do good* in the short time we all have on the planet.
We think of coaching as a way of partnering to create highly customized and collaborative, just-in-time adult learning and leadership development. Leaders who have experienced coaching usually begin to listen differently, to ask questions differently, and to keep a laser focus on agreed-upon priorities, competencies, competitiveness, and performance. Their teams then join the learning. The results can be impressive and contagious, and the ROI compelling.

Like you, we know that talented employees are looking for work that matters. This usually means finding a sense of purpose and service. And they are also seeking opportunities at work for personal and professional development. If both elements are not present, those employees are more likely to change companies than they are to simply change jobs within the company. The old saying still seems to be true that *talented people join great companies, and they leave bad managers.*

Some Anecdotal Feedback: One Company's Experience of CFL

At the conclusion of one of our first rounds of CFL at Microsoft, I asked the participants: *Do you think this company of yours will make more money, have more fun, and do more good because you guys have invested this time in becoming coaching leaders?*

Their answers (coming mostly all at once):

- *We'll listen better and take better risks.*
- *We'll ask better questions and be more innovative.*
- *We'll take criticism better.*
- *We'll course correct faster.*
- *We'll argue about the right things, but more kindly.*
- *We'll probably stay around longer.*

Then I think someone dropped a mic.

SeattleCoach is the "craft brewery of leadership coaching." In everything we do, our goal is to start with world-class ingredients: our content, our process, and cohorts of people like you. Along the way we stay accessible and responsive, and we leave a coaching community of "Connection, Curiosity, and Challenge" in our wake. We charge for our work, but the affection is free.

In the SeattleCoach Stash PDF: Books and articles from our most enduringly favorite coaching thought leaders.[36]

Appendix: Article II

Preparing and Leading a Meeting Like a Coach

We all know that sometimes "check-in" is simply a time of pleasantries while a team waits for the latecomers to arrive. But as the leader becomes fluent in their use of the **Coaching Leader's Arena**, their meetings change. Whether your meeting is (1) a huddle to address urgent and tactical obstacles and opportunities or to clarify expectations, or (2) a higher-level strategic meeting, or (3) a less frequent, equally crucial team-building meeting, think about this acronym:

ASK US

Anticipate as you build the agenda

What's top of mind for you? Your hunches? Your outcomes? (Same question in advance to everyone who will attend your meeting.)

Set the table and make it worth being on time

In any gathering, personal or professional, we know the difference between being "expected" and being "wanted." Mark the moment like a host.

Know the power of your respect, energy, acknowledgment, & listening

Good-news-bad-news: leaders are contagious.

Use prompts to help people identify what matters, what needs to be said

What's distracting you? What's top of mind? What are the outcomes that will make this a good meeting? What are the questions we need to answer? Ideas you want to bring up?

Set time limits for "check-in"—leave time to return to a longer conversation

When a team member brings up something big during check-in, call a time out and add their item to the larger agenda to which you'll return after everyone has checked in. Checking-in well takes time if people are working at Level 3, but if you and your team are well-prepared and even unhurried, it's not unusual for a great check-in to become seamless with the larger shared agenda.

Appendix: Article III

Using Assessments and Inventories in Individual and Team Coaching

Train up a child in the way he should go and when he is old, he will not depart from it. —Proverbs 22:6

(Patty's long-winded paraphrase: Parents, inaugurate your child onto the path of a good life by appreciating their unique dispositions and strengths—their singular characteristics. This is a course from which people, as a general rule, will not deviate.)

If you're a good coach, any assessment is a supplement, not a substitute. As with any coaching tool, the purpose of an assessment is to help people have a conversation with themselves and then with you and others about their "way." In choosing which assessment to use, ask yourself what this individual or team wants to become more aware of, measure, or inspire.

Do you want to get clarity about a person's true and emerging strengths, values, and interests? Information about their aptitudes, temperaments, and ambitions?

- *Are you working with a team in which the members are ready to leverage their relationships toward greater development, cohesiveness, shared values, and even comfort with disagreement? Maybe it's a team that will even be brave and kind enough to help some members leave for a better fit.*

A negative consequence of some diagnostic assessments is what Carol Dweck has called "a fixed mindset."[37] We've all heard it: *"I'm red energy! Deal with it!" "I'm an SF—don't make me do conflict!"* or *"I'm a C—just let me take care of the data and details."*

With as assessment that instead sheds light on personal strengths and sense of purpose or calling, you are able to challenge and support the person or team you're coaching to apply those core advantages to their agenda and aspirations. Of course, it's why we asked you to take the VIA Character Strengths Survey[38] at the beginning of **CFL**. You'll remember that this assessment is part of a strong longitudinal study, but you don't need special training to use it.

Once the person I'm coaching and I have begun to identify their *signature strengths*, I ask questions like:

- *What happens when you use those strengths and values well? How could you do that with this issue we're talking about today? What would a 10-percent shift look like in that meeting tomorrow?*
- *Could you ever overuse them?*
- *What happens just before you get mad or sad?*

In addition to the VIA, I use the following tools to help individuals and teams gain a sense of exploring, and even crafting, their lives.

Both can be valuable as pre-work to rich conversations. If you are a graduate of **CFL**, consider yourself trained in the use of these narrative SeattleCoach instruments. I've place both in **The SeattleCoach Stash.** Just leave in my copyright and contact information.

Appendix: Article IV

Knowing Your DATA[ii]

There are a zillion ways to know yourself better. In addition to assessments and inventories, try thinking through these four categories. Before anything else, the role of any assessment is for your coachee—or you! to better understand his or her own story, hopes, and resources. Of course, assessments also help us as coaches to shape our curiosity and questions. Think of this as an intuitive and emotional exercise as much as an analytical one.

And take a few notes on the worksheet below.

Desires   What do you feel passionately about? If $$ were no object, what would you do? What do other people love about what you do—and would they (or do they) gladly compensate you for? Other than money, how do you like to be compensated? What did you love as a kid that you still love?

Abilities   This is the stuff that tends to show up on a traditional résumé. What goes on your list of unique skills, training, professional capabilities, experience, etc.? For example: managing projects, information technology, writing, speaking, leading teams in energetically solving problems, working with your hands, co-creating agreements, etc. This is the subject matter expertise (SME) you've spent years learning and refining.

As you think about your Abilities, you'll notice that some bring energy while others may feel ready to retire.

Temperament This is the Core of who you are. I expand "temperament" to mean a few other things, like:

- Knowing how to understand and use your values (your time and $$)
- Knowing how you like to solve problems—and how patient you you can be when they persist for awhile
- How you're likely to behave in conflict or when you're stressed or exhausted
- Knowing what happens when you're physically, emotionally, socially at the "top of your game"
- And what happens when you're mobilizing for action
- Maybe what makes you tiresome and irritating to be around
- Or, even better, what makes you wonderful to be around
- Or how you remember why you've chosen this path—and how you re-find your empathy

Assets   These are your unique life advantages that can deepen the work you do and the conversations and situations you get into. For example:

- You grew up with or have become fluent in a second or third language
- You have a faith tradition that informs your approach to life and relationships
- A good grown-up appeared in your life when you were a teenager, right when you needed them

- You were born in another country
- You belong to a minority group
- You have a family member with a disability
- You're in solid recovery from an addiction
- You were an Eagle Scout or a Merit Scholar
- You've experienced a great loss
- You are a parent—or grandparent

Thanks to William Bridges, who wrote early and often about transitions, for first suggesting the DATA acronym. Now use the next page as a brainstorming tool.

Your DATA Worksheet

Desires	Abilities	Temperament	Assets

Appendix: Article V

Your Vocáre Compass

One Way to Soul-Search and Self-Coach Over Time

To journey without being changed is to be a nomad. To change without journeying is to be a chameleon.
To journey and be transformed by the journey is to be a pilgrim. —Mark Nepo

The big break for me was deciding that this was my life. —Jon Stewart

I quite like that I haven't done "good enough" yet. —Sir Paul McCartney (age 78)

I insist on a lot of time being spent, almost every day, to just sit and think. —Warren Buffett

Experience is a hard teacher because she gives the test first, the lesson afterward.
—Vern Law, a pitcher for the Pittsburgh Pirates in the 1950s and 1960s

I think midlife is when the universe gently places her hands upon your shoulders, pulls you close,
and whispers in your ear: "I'm not screwing around. It's time." —Brené Brown

I've noticed through the years that the thoughtful people I know and love seem to always be curious about a few questions, each of which can seem pretty fresh:

- *How do I attend to my journey so that my gifts, strengths, training, and values and legacy are maximized?*
- *In my few decades on the planet, how do I pay attention to my unfolding sense of purpose?*
- *And, other than money, how do I like to be compensated?*

The English word "vocation" has grown a little coolly practical, but through the centuries, the Latin verb that inspired it—*vocáre*—has carried the essential meaning of being called to a specific kind of work, to a craft, or maybe as an apprentice to a master. For some, a sense of calling is a spiritual aspiration. For others it's about "fit" and the paradox you've probably experienced at times of effortless hard work.

Theories abound about how one succeeds in this treasure hunt: Is it a divine epiphany? Or logging "10,000 hours?" Or "following your bliss?"

My theory is that it's mostly about paying attention to your life and getting useful feedback from good people. It's an iterative process. Like checking the heading on a compass. Like keeping an eye on your personal North Star.

For decades, those thoughtful people I know and love have seemed to see their lives as a deep stewardship (another old word); they are people who are very serious about examining their gifts and abilities and motivations—and the question of their "calling." From thoughtful twenty-somethings to reflective mid-career professionals, to the wise elders who regularly tell me, "I'm not done yet!," they are very serious about finding and refining their path for the limited number of years they have left on the planet.

Your Vocáre Compass is an exercise that might be key to your own continuous contentment in life. Maybe it reflects your own evolving True North.

What I started to notice . . .

Through the years, restless coachees kept showing up in my offices at Lake Union. Each was ready for a course correction. And I started to notice patterns.

Some had been paid well for years for their world-class expertise. But many had just experienced a birthday that ends in a zero, and, though they were grateful for their hard-won expertise and for their financial stability, they had begun thinking about their sense of purpose and legacy.

Others were world-class in their artistic abilities or non-profit work. These people already had a deep sense of purpose and legacy, and they too were grateful for their hard-won expertise. But having also experienced a birthday that ends in a zero (midlife does seem to focus the mind), they had the realization that they were broke.

Each one of these coachees was satisfied with only two of the following three core incentives. Each one sensed that it was time to check their contentment—their personal compass heading.

I work with leaders and coaches who are ready to check their heading. Usually they're restless. Maybe they are paid well to do something that they're not getting better at or enjoying like they used to. Maybe they want to find a way to make a living doing something that gives them a deeper sense of satisfaction and contribution. Maybe they are ready to cultivate an area of potential mastery or income with which they've only experimented (but for which they've usually been thanked).

Think of Your Vocáre Compass as having three core incentives— and a True North where they intersect . . .

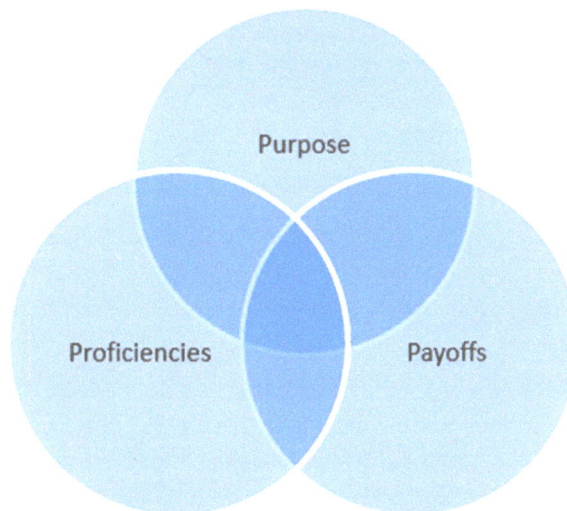

1. Proficiencies

What is the work that, up to this point in your career, you've gotten pretty good at? Maybe you love it, maybe you love parts of it. What is the craft, the subject matter expertise (SME) for which you are already known even as you begin to embrace your identity as a professional coach or coaching leader? How will you use your SME as a coach? How does your SME inform the niche you might want to serve? How does your SME inform your Level 3 questioning and listening? Could your SME be something around which you'd build a workshop—where you introduce, explain, and illustrate a bite-sized chunk of great content and then coach a group or a team as they metabolize it?

2. Purpose

If Circle #1 is about your "What," Circle #2 is about your "Why." Maybe you notice it at the end of a very satisfying day in which you know you have contributed, served, and lived out your big strengths and values. You lost track of time a little. Maybe you know deeply that you have developed or championed greater efficiency or order or delight or a team that works well together. Maybe you lead an organization that employs hundreds of people who love what they do and act like its owners. If you have a spiritual tradition or practice, your sense of purpose will feel aligned with it. There is almost always a connection between prosperity and having a clear sense of purpose or even calling. Maybe you don't follow your bliss, but you do keep it in sight.

3. Payoffs

Speaking of prosperity, along the way, you begin to notice opportunities that appear. What might people pay you to do—gladly and even generously? What could you be one of the best in town at? And what does great compensation look like for you? **And other than money, how do you like to be compensated?**

Each circle is crucial, interdependent, and, by itself, not enough

And each one may seek your attention in different ways, and at different times. As you explore and attend to each circle, the compass gets dynamic. Your sense of fit resonates: expertise, service, and prosperity. Proficiencies. Purpose. Payoffs. As with following any compass, where you start is not where you'll land, and course corrections are continuous: your intuition gets restless; you stop and check, and maybe backtrack or sprint or stop to savor a spectacular vista.

Now look at the circles again. Start with the one that is most personally compelling.

Circle #1: Proficiencies

Again, this circle represents the work that you know you do well. Most of us after a decade or so of work begin to think about what we want more of and less of. As you think through the abilities, assets, education, experience, personal traits, and gifts that belong to you, some will inspire you more than others. Pay attention to stories you love to tell about your work and how you've gotten to know what you know. *How'd you do that? What's working? And how can you do more of that?*

Circle #2: Purpose

This circle represents what you feel strongly about, or why you work so hard. Maybe your attention turns to where you've always had a sense of special satisfaction or contribution in your work or because of your work. You provide an income and an example that matters. You do the work and you don't cheat. If you have a sense of spirituality and stewardship about your time on the planet, maybe that comes to your attention. *What are the compliments that mean the most to you? Who do they come from?*

Circle #3: Payoffs

This circle speaks to what spells freedom to you: a number probably comes to mind. Write it down. But also ask yourself, *What would people pay me to do?* And, *Once the money is ok, how else do I like to be compensated?* It's probably about being able to have choices and autonomy and the ability to explore and produce: maybe you like a strong team with an affirming leader, or being your own boss, or traveling a lot, or not, or being acknowledged publicly for your craftsmanship, or making innovation practical, or being trusted with a flexible work schedule. Write down some very clear specifics. Notice answers that integrate your life and your work.

Daniel Goleman says in his book *Focus*[39] that the much-heralded 10,000 hours rule is *"only half true. If you are a duffer at golf, say, and make the same mistakes every time you try a certain swing or putt, 10,000 hours of practicing that error will not improve your game. You'll still be a duffer, albeit an older one."*

And I would add that if you like the work so much that in addition to the hours you add focus, tolerance for failure, tweaking, and the risk required to increase your limits, your True North begins to emerge.

Bonus Points: Your Personal 360

As you use these questions to listen to your life, you may want to bring in a few consultants—people who know you well and are in your corner. Try asking them to talk with you about the following questions:

- *"What do you see as my main skills and areas of expertise? What else?"*
- *"Where do you see me getting most focused and enthusiastic?"*
- *"What do you think the world would gladly pay me—or thank me—to do more of?"*
- *Or simply ask them to talk to you about a time when they saw you at your best.*

The idea, of course, is to listen to your life—and to both your restlessness and contentment.

Both have an iterative magnetic pull. Your strengths, opportunities, aspirations, results—and even your restlessness—will help you to know how to listen, both to your own life as a coach. You will become increasingly clear about where the circles get most vivid and complementary—and to make a habit of listening for the rest of your life.

In the SeattleCoach Stash: *Listen to my six minutes on Your Vocáre Compass.*[jj]

And, for a lovely example, I've added the very creative Vocáre Compass *from SeattleCoach Nina Brandes.*[kk]

Appendix: Article VI

"Getting to Whoosh"

Rowing Metaphor #1

A 13-foot oar hangs in the main meeting room in my offices on Lake Union in Seattle. It was used for years in the racing shells rowing past, through the Montlake Cut and into Lake Washington. For 10 years I rowed the "eights" competitively and practiced the lessons of the beautiful sport. The old oar in my office reminds me of how those lessons apply today as I coach the men and women and teams who meet under it. These are a few I will never forget:

1. My rowing coaches helped me to value consistent, disciplined, inspired effort even more than breakthroughs or epiphanies. That meant three or four mornings a week at 5:00 a.m. with my friends, usually in the cold and dark. The lesson: Determine what you long for and commit to it. Having allies that are equally committed and who, over time, become your friends makes it more fun.

2. Racing shells that are powered by balanced rowers are designed to go fast. New rowers are strong and enthusiastic, but they are tempted to wrestle the oar and those sliding seats. They will soon join the rhythm of the other rowers, but for now they check the momentum of the boat that just wants to go fast. When teams are just forming, they tend to get tired and wet and not go fast. But as they learn to cooperate—with the boat and the water, with their own bodies and with each other—they learn the simple, strong rhythm of push and glide. Even when they are pulling hard, veteran rowers make it look elegant. The lesson: Look and listen for the rhythm and "the run." Learn to find it and repeat it.

3. Resistance is part of what makes a boat go fast. When rowers drop their blades into the water at just the right moment and then quickly engage their strength to move against the resistance of the water, the boat surges. And with every stroke, the momentum is more in their favor. The lesson: Resistance does not have to be the enemy if you can get the ratio right between the challenge and the glide.

4. As the momentum turns in a race, the temptation is to start looking around. Rowers may face backward, but they can clearly see their place in the race. Like all competitors, they watch, asking, *Where is the competition? How are they doing? Who is ahead? Am I strong enough? Can I keep this up? Starting to get tired, and here comes the sprint.* The lesson: Focus on your own race. Love the competition. You are consistent and disciplined, trusting yourself, your boat, and the other rowers.

5. And maybe you hear it. Whoosh. Whoosh. Whoosh. And then maybe you feel it. Veteran rowers call it "swing." From a dead stop, your strokes have brought up the speed and lifted your boat through the water. As you come forward for each new stroke, the wheels on your seats roll evenly, not breaking the momentum but cooperating with it. Push and glide. Crisp. Clean. Elusive. The lesson: Momentum will take on a life of its own.

Parts of the race are steady and not very glamorous. And then you burst into a sprint to the finish line. Which strokes win the race? None of the rowers could say for sure. What they will tell you is that in the final 500 meters, if they are rowing well, it is a combination of skill, trust, challenge, strength, conditioning, cooperation, rhythm, balance, effort, and magic as the boat runs beneath them. Like competitive rowers, people who are working hard to refocus their lives, work, and teams engage all of those things too, usually with very little fanfare. But when the magic of "whoosh" begins to take hold, they know it. And the magic is compelling.

Appendix: Article VII

"A Rowing Coach Has to Decide"

Rowing Metaphor #2

When a rowing coach puts together a competitive eight, she asks her rowers to compete for their seats: *Who should be in this boat? Who should be in which seat?* She knows that each seat has its own requirements and psychology. She asks the same questions any good leader asks—questions of strength, skill, and grit are pretty easy to measure. But veteran coaches also ask an intuitive question about fit:

Do I choose the eight best? Or the best eight? *Which eight can row as one? Each rower unique, committed, and connected.*

"The eight best? The best eight?" Guess which crew usually wins.

About the Author

As a leader, facilitator, and coach of leaders, Patricia (Patty) Burgin has advised and mentored thousands of individuals and teams toward better performance, communication, and meaning.

Following stints in the international leadership of a Christian nonprofit, as a conference speaker, as a tour leader in the former Soviet Union, and as a licensed marriage and family therapist, Patty founded SeattleCoach® in 2003 and began to coach and facilitate exclusively in 2005. In 2008, she launched the SeattleCoach Professional Training and Development Company, which is credentialed by the industry-standard International Coaching Federation (ICF). And in 2015, as the demand for organizational coaching leadership grew, "Coaching for Leaders" became a reality.

Whether through a class or a keynote, Patty values insight creation as the crucial component of content delivery. "I love it when my brain lights up," she says. "And it's even better when everyone else's brains light up." She works with an approach that is warm, practical, innovative, direct, playful, and generous.

She holds two master's degrees—one in theology and a second in applied behavioral science—and has joined the top 4 percent of credentialed coaches worldwide to have been awarded the title of Master Certified Coach by the ICF.

A native of the Pacific Northwest, Patty loves almost everything about it: the water, the coast, the mountains, the IPAs, and *"not having to squint as much as Californians do."* During her freshman year at Oregon State University, she was honored to be named "Smart Ass of the Year" by members of her sorority. She lives near the Seattle Zoo with her partner, Dr. Kari—a veterinarian—plus Lambchop, Beep, Gromit, Winston, and Clementine.

With Patty's background as a competitive rower and past president of Interlochen Rowing Club in Seattle, she sometimes takes executive teams out on the water with her. When a team sits together in a racing shell (60' x 18"), the experience quickly produces soggy metaphors and boatloads of team learning.

Patty's faith informs her life and work, helping her explore how human brains and relationships flourish, how we make sense of the tough stuff, and how we live out those big what's-it-all-about questions that we share through the arcs of our lives. She thinks excellent coaching is like grace: rarely intrusive, usually disruptive, more nuanced than announced, and just as much about **how** as **what**.

www.ingramcontent.com/pod-product-compliance
Lightning Source LLC
Chambersburg PA
CBHW050908210326
41597CB00002B/64